Digital Supply Chains

Thomas Mrozek and *Daniel Seitz* are both partner at *h&z* and are responsible for supply chain management. Mrozek's specialization is making supply chains future-proof, and he works with major corporations and medium-sized businesses to make sustainable improvements to service. Seitz is the co-founder of *h&z* Supply Chain Innovation Forums. He works to make businesses and organizations reach higher levels of performance by developing innovative concepts.

Kai-Uwe Gundermann, Senior Expert and Project Leader at *h&z*, combines expert knowledge with practical experience for supply chain management. His emphasis is on planning, logistics, production and operating model optimization.

Matthias Dicke is a consultant and part of Supply Chain Practice at *h&z*. In his capacity as digital native and a member of Generation Y, he is particularly interested in working with clients to institute new practices along the supply chain.

Enjoy your book whenever and wherever you like!

WITH THIS BOOK YOU HAVE ALSO PURCHASED THE EBOOK EDITION

1. Go to www.campus.de/ebookinside.

2. To obtain your free ebook, please enter the following **download code** into the space below.

   »E-Book inside«: AXVJN-UPXV6-Z7ZY4

3. Select a **format** (MOBI/Kindle, EPUB or PDF).

4. Fill in the form with your email address and click the button at the end. You will then receive your **personal download link** via email.

Thomas Mrozek
Daniel Seitz
Kai-Uwe Gundermann
Matthias Dicke

DIGITAL SUPPLY CHAINS

A Practitioner's Guide
to Successful Digitalization

Campus Verlag
Frankfurt/New York

Bibliographic Information published by the Deutsche Nationalbibliothek.
The Deutsche Nationalbibliothek lists this publication in the
Deutsche Nationalbibliografie; detailed bibliographic data are
available in the Internet at http://dnb.d-nb.de.

ISBN 978-3-593-51205-1 Print
ISBN 978-3-593-44397-3 E-Book (PDF)
ISBN 978-3-593-44396-6 E-Book (EPUB)

Copyright © 2020 Campus Verlag GmbH, Frankfurt/Main
Cover illustration: © Shutterstock: Artistdesign29
Cover design: Guido Klütsch, Köln
Typesetting: Publikations Atelier, Dreieich
Interial illustration blockchain: © Shutterstock: a-images
Printing office and bookbinder: Beltz Grafische Betriebe GmbH, Bad Langensalza
Printed in Germany
www.campus.de
www.press.uchicago.edu

Contents

Part 3
Leverage Enablers for Supply Chain Functions

PART 1

Chapter 1
General Introduction

To ensure easy reading, we added some icons for you

The *magnifying glass* marks industry insights.	
The *dialog symbol* flags interviews and quotes from conversations which we conducted with industry experts and academics.	
The *future vision symbol* highlights the vision for digital SCM on the respective topic.	
The *direction icon* will tell you where you can find a step-by-step guide on how to progress towards the final vision.	
Finally, the *survival kit* provides you with a checklist of the most important points in order for you to be able to kick-start actions.	

Overview of Interviews

"Bring your clients to the digital world—They expect it from you."

Martin Zehnder, COO, PALFINGER AG

"People are the most important success factor in digital projects."

Roland Becker, Managing Director, GLX Logistics

"The development of digital supply chains is an evolution rather than a revolution."

Peter Dressler, Senior Director Logistics, Infineon

"There's no quick fix when it comes to transformation."

Jacob Gorm Larsen, Director of Digital Procurement, Maersk Group

"Digitalization cannot be avoided."

Hartwig Meinen, Managing Director Logistics,
Elflein Spedition & Transport GmbH

"The goal is to create awareness at management level first."

Thorsten Rosenberg, Executive Vice President & Head of Global Supply Chain,
BSH Hausgeräte GmbH

"It will become increasingly important for people to retrain and learn new skills."

Alexander Gisdakis, Former Head of HR Leadership Culture, Siemens AG

"There's no hype when it comes to digitalization—it's a fundamentally important topic."

Erik Wirsing, Vice President Global Innovation, DB Schenker

"Culture has come to occupy a more prominent place in today's companies than it used to."

Simon Sagmeister, Founder and CEO, The Culture Institute

We would also like to thank the following people for their active support, contribution, valuable expertise and shared experiences:

- *Simon Sagmeister* (The Culture Institute)
- *Professor Doctor of Engineering Guido H. Baltes*, University of Constance
- *Philipp Smole*, Executive Vice President Corporate Incubator PALFINGER 21ˢᵗ
- *Dr Christian Rohrdantz*, Managing Director, and *Johannes Häussler*, Data Scientist, Vidatics GmbH
- *Dr Maximilian Hausmann*, Senior Manager, *Dr Elena Michel*, Manager Data Analytics, rpc—The Retail Performance Company

Acknowledgement

Supply chain management is without question deeply affected by the disruptive forces of a modern organization, positively as well as negatively. Between Advanced Analytics and AI, agile role models and autonomous warehouses a senior executive is often in danger of losing track in the digital jungle.

In these exciting times, with their many turning points, h&z aims to share insights around digital supply chains, their application in business and the so vital transformation to successfully prepare organizations for this challenge. This book provides insights into best practices of current supply chain and how CSOs apply technologies and advancements. It also makes daring forecasts about how processes and leadership must be designed so that the digital transformation does not fail in its infancy, but leads to a truly agile organization.

Fortunately, we didn't have to do all this on our own. We would like to thank all contributors from leading industry organizations for their opinions and insights about supply chain management. We would also like to thank the entire h&z family, whose patience and dedication made this book possible.

Bring your clients to the digital world— They expect it from you: Letter from a COO

Dear digital practitioners,

We are in the age of digital transformation. Our lifestyles, the way we work, the way we communicate, and the way we shop are changing and they will never be the same again. One implication of these changes is that those of us in the business of supplying products and services need to adapt swiftly to the rapidly changing requirements of our customers otherwise they will look elsewhere.

At PALFINGER we are innovating and driving transformation to shape the future for us and our clients to make sure they stay with us. In our new digitalization program, we are pooling our digital competencies as well as adopting new approaches to the products and services we supply, all for the benefit of our customers. In addition, it is our ambition that the digital assistance systems and tools we use not only make work processes easier, improve support, and support cost-effectiveness—they also make every day work safer.

These are a few examples of our digital solutions, spanning customer solutions to improved operations:

TELEMATICS: Collect data in real time and turn it into value-add for our customers which can be for example displayed in a web portal so that fleet managers and users always know the current condition of our equipment. This minimizes unplanned machine downtimes and optimizes spare-part management.

FLEET AND OPERATOR MONITORING: We developed digital tools that boost the efficiency and productivity of our fleet loader cranes. The platform shows which machines are in use and where, and how long they have been operating. The system enables site managers to optimize crane use and loading processes and therefore ensures that the fleet is fully connected and all relevant job data is delivered where it is needed while the operator monitor supports the operation in the field or construction site with relevant data.

SAFETY SOLUTIONS: The theft of any of our equipment leads to drastic delays and cost increases for the customers using it, which is why we have developed systems to make sure the risk is dramatically decreased. If machines are moved without authorization, the customer is automatically informed. This not only considerably reduces the risk of theft, it also has the added benefit of potentially reducing insurance premiums.

In parallel to these customer-focused services, we have launched the first technology-based projects to improve certain internal SCM operations, including:

- intelligent loading assistant systems for inbound logistics
- traceability of production material
- connected production plants
- production automation
- paperless production
- and predictive maintenance through fleet monitoring

I am happy to share with you here a few corporate and personal lessons I have learnt in the process of PALFINGER's digital transformation. My hope is that this could be instrumental in helping some other companies with their journeys to digitalization.

BUILD UP A DIGITAL ECOSYSTEM: With the rapid pace of technological change we see today it is nearly impossible to stay tuned to the most recent and advanced digital solutions on your own. This is why it is important to build up partnership networks within and outside your ecosystem. We founded PALFINGER 21st as incubator, which is an umbrella capturing new possibilities, opportunities and ideas. It is supposed to enable unconventional approaches and fresh fields of expertise. It is a distinct business area that faces up to new technologies and promotes radical ideas with the potential to change our business. It is worth considering setting up a similar kind of organization to help your own company. It should aim to filter out the best ideas, those that would work as part of your company's digital transformation, and to identify opportunities early on. We established an environment in which our colleagues can experiment together, make mistakes, learn from them—and develop the products and services of tomorrow through a profound understanding of our customers.

One more example of an activity that helped to enlarge our ecosystem and bring in new ideas was Austria's largest hackathon in 2017, which the PALFINGER Group hosted[1]. More than 100 participants, grouped in 24 teams, competed for the chance to further develop their ideas.

The participants were challenged to come up with ideas for seven subject areas:

- virtual reality, augmented reality, mixed reality
- intelligent loading assistant for inbound logistics
- predictive maintenance through fleet monitoring
- production automation
- digital assistance systems
- 3D printing within production
- and PALFINGER as a service

The three winning teams gave short elevator pitches, supported by videos, simulations and prototypes, that aimed to convince the jury about their ideas. They are now developing their solutions together with PALFINGER.

GET THE BASICS RIGHT: If you want to make full use of digital potentials, you must first have a strong IT backbone in place. We are currently running an SAP S/4 HANA project in all our major sites (not all our sites have SAP in place) in a concerted attempt to get uniform and consistent data pools across all regions and sites. Before the decision was made to implement this new ERP system, we carried out a large process excellence project to define standardized projects across the board. I am sure that you agree that it does not make a lot of sense to implement a standard ERP system without having harmonized your process landscape beforehand. You can of course use digital solutions to achieve some momentum where a fully integrated data lake is not needed. But at the end of the day, you need a common IT backbone to be able to scale up successful pilots across the board.

STICK TO YOUR TRAITS: There are numerous examples out there of companies that have transformed their business models from being pure hardware manufacturers to system integrators, where they have orchestrated the whole digital ecosystem using the digital solutions available to them. I am convinced that this transformation is only possible if you have the financial power to make the necessary long-term investments. It might, however, be a better idea to stick to your traits and focus on niche segments and applications where you can win the battle, and also prepare yourself for the big solution or disruption. We have therefore ensured that our products are connectable and platform-ready so they can exchange data with our partners within our ecosystem whatever platform solutions are used.

ACCEPT TWO SPEEDS WITHIN THE COMPANY: Companies with a long history normally have different maturity levels for process and data quality and IT systems between different regions or organizational units. This is also the case with PALFINGER, with 21 acquisitions over the last decade that have operated as independent units. My advice is to go through a three-step approach to fully address these challenges.

STEP 1: Bring all units and regions to the same levels in terms of IT systems and process excellence.

STEP 2: Foster innovative ideas within the more mature units with an explore, test, and implement approach. Identify proof-of-concept projects and pilots so they are ready to be scaled up once more units and regions have achieved higher levels of process and data management excellence.

STEP 3: Once you have closed existing excellence gaps between the units or regions and you have a harmonized process landscape, the next step is to scale up successful pilots. By doing so you can build up a self-financing project pipeline, where successfully scaled pilots will generate savings to finance other pilots or proof-of-concept projects that are in the pipeline.

In general, I would advise you to have a solid framework to support digitalization. Based on the strength of this framework, you can define your ambition level and select individual initiatives from your innovation funnel on the basis of what contribution they will make to achieving the next level of digital maturity.

DON'T FORGET THE PEOPLE: It is imperative that you have the right culture in place to be successful in digitalization. PALFINGER 21st works as a fully independent start-up but it has strong links to PALFINGER so that ideas and project funnels can be aligned with technological capabilities and the overall corporate strategy. For example, it works as a catalyst, but in close collaboration with the mother company, to bring agile ways of working and design thinking approaches to areas such as products, software development, and digital projects in general. Our new organization strengthened cross-functional collaboration and led to a new office concept. Both, together with the fundamental organizational changes we have made, play a vital role in further developing our corporate culture.

MY CONCLUSION: My last piece of advice is that it is important that you find your own way through digital transformation. There is no prescriptive path, no one-size-fits-all solution for digitalization. You should learn from the successes and failures of other companies that have already been through this transformation and when possible, reach out to them and exchange views. Our experience tells us that other companies are open to sharing knowledge. Many companies are more or less in the same situation and depend on external stimuli in such digitally disruptive times.

I hope that you find the best approach for your company and develop a strategic vision to match the level of your digital ambition.

Best regards
Martin Zehnder
COO PALFINGER AG

ABOUT MARTIN ZEHNDER: Born in 1967, Martin Zehnder joined the PALFINGER Group in 2005 as Global Manufacturing Manager for the manufacturing plants. Since January 2008, he has been responsible for the worldwide manufacturing and assembly area as a member of the Executive Board responsible for Production, and since September 2017 for Product Line Management, R&D, Purchasing, Safety & Quality and the Executive Projects Process Excellence and Turnkey Solutions.

ABOUT PALFINGER GROUP: For many years PALFINGER has been one of the world's leading manufacturers of innovative lifting solutions for use on commercial vehicles and in the maritime sector. As a multinational group headquartered in Bergheim, Austria, the PALFINGER Group, which has more than 11,000 employees, generated total sales of more than €1.6bn in 2018.

PART 2

ENABLERS FOR FUTURE SUPPLY CHAINS

Chapter 2.1
Building blocks of the Digital Supply Chain
Thomas Mrozek
Key technology trends

Introduction

 Digital technologies are ubiquitous in our daily lives at home, at work and in the services we use to support our lifestyle. We use our mobile devices to place orders online, for communication, and as a tool to make critical business decisions whether we're in the office or on the go. It's impossible to imagine life without them, but how will technology continue to impact and change our jobs, our day-to-day lives and the routines we are used to? One thing we can say for certain is that when they are used correctly, digital solutions open the door to improved speed and efficiency, and whoever working in supply chain management (SCM) is not interested in such improvements?

"The development towards digital supply chains is an evolution rather than a revolution. Many ideas and concepts have existed for many years. However, it's only today that technology is evolving in a direction that makes digital solutions feasible and realizable. This is the case because of increasing processing memory, Artificial Intelligence approaches and upcoming technologies like 5G."

Peter Dressler, Senior Director Logistics, Infineon

In this chapter we will review nine digital technologies, some established and some emerging, and the effects they will have on supply chain management. Together these key technologies form the foundation for digital supply chains and have the potential to change the way we operate. We will provide an essential overview of the nine key technologies, the highly sought-after benefits inherent in their use, and how they can be applied along the supply chain.

Key terms and their definitions

First, it's important that we define and clarify the main terms that will be used throughout this chapter and others.

Digital Supply Chain Management

Digital supply chain management is classic supply chain management with added information and communication technologies that utilize data in order to gain deeper insights. A digital supply chain leverages intelligence and know-how embedded in physical objects and matches this intelligence with internal and external data through automation and connectivity along the supply chain. It allows us to access computed information and process results anytime and anywhere to make evaluated and business-driven decisions.

These information and communication technologies are used to integrate all flows of materials, products, people and information across different logistics channels, from raw material to end customer. The aim is to meet customer expectations with increased efficiency in terms of cost, synergies, sustainability and effectiveness.

A digital supply chain means you can use intelligent processes that, for example, link real-time inventory, customer interactions with products, parcel service data and Internet of Things (IoT) technology.

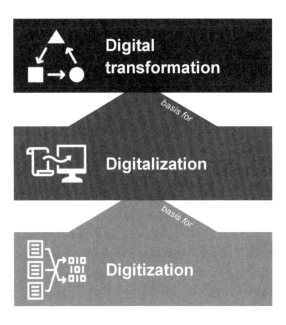

Figure 1: Digitization, digitalization and digital transformation

Digitization

Digitization is the process of creating a digital (bits and bytes) version of analog or physical materials such as paper documents, microfilm images, photographs, sounds, video and more.

Converting something non-digital (for example, health records, location data, identity cards) into a digital format means they can then be stored and accessed by a computing system. Digitizing information from analog assets or technical products extends their applicability beyond what they were originally intended for. Hence, these are also referred to as smart (intelligent) products.

Digitalization

"There's no hype when it comes to digitalization—it's a fundamentally important topic. I strongly believe that companies that are not currently prepared for digitalization, or are just starting to get ready, will face dramatically difficult problems."

Erik Wirsing, Vice President Global Innovation, DB Schenker

According to Gartner, "Digitalization is the use of digital technologies to change a business model and provide new revenue and value-producing opportunities," or "the process of moving to a digital business." Although this may be stating the obvious, what is not so clear is what is meant by a digital business. So, for the sake of clarity, when the term digital business is used throughout this book, it refers to the creation of new business designs by blurring the digital and physical worlds. It also refers to connectivity, integration and collaboration between business partners who use IT systems instead of paper for their processes (from planning to design).[1]

In essence, digitalization automates material processes and tasks and changes the way people interact.

A simple example of loading a truck can illustrate a lot about digitalization. Before digitalization, the truck driver would have needed to stop at the factory gate to submit loading papers before being told at which ramp to park the truck for loading. After loading he would have needed to drive towards the gate again, get the loading papers stamped and approved before exiting the factory premises.

With the use of digital technologies the process for the truck driver changes significantly. First, the truck's number plate is scanned and the ramp information is displayed immediately on his mobile device. After loading, the truck driver sees that documents were electronically transmitted (digitized) onto the truck loading paper manager. Then, while approaching the gate, RFID tags automatically indicate the weight and quantity of loaded goods to the responsible officer at the gate and the exit procedures are released. Finally, the gate opens and the truck leaves.

The benefits of the digitalized procedure include less time spent on the yard, faster turnaround, and fewer errors in documentation, to name a few. Of course, this example can be extended to include digitalization of additional technologies like picking or loading automation and autonomous loading vehicles or even trucks.

Digital Transformation

Digital transformation refers to the strategic and prioritized alteration of business activities, processes, competencies and models to fully leverage the changes and opportunities of digital technologies and their impacts across society. The main drivers of digital transformation are information technologies such as networking, hardware and digital applications.[2]

The Digital Supply Chain Pillars

Digitally transforming the supply chain requires a clear understanding of how to use the five building blocks (see below) that support digital technologies and their applications. These building blocks depend on each other and cannot be seen in isolation. For example, analytics relies heavily on data but also on connectivity and the digital ecosystem, while autonomous driving relies on all of the building blocks.

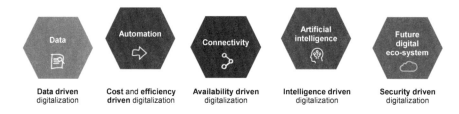

Figure 2: Digital supply chain pillars

Let's review the building blocks one by one:

DATA: With the increasing complexity of global supply chains processes are increasingly data driven. The processing of structured and unstructured data is the foundation of improvements to digital supply chains.

AUTOMATION refers to the variety of applications, ranging from highly automated processes, affordable robotics, to intelligent and self-directed systems, that perform complex tasks.

CONNECTIVITY deals with the interconnectivity of goods, processes and people through wireless technology, sensors and geo-localization. Connectivity also helps with collaboration by enabling flexibility on how, when and where people work and access systems and information. This also drives new ways of working and collaborating such as augmented and virtual reality.

ARTIFICIAL INTELLIGENCE is a domain of computer science that enables machines to sense and reason, so they can, for example, recognize patterns and give predictions. Machine learning is a subset of Artificial Intelligence (AI) and consists of algorithms which can improve their predictions if they are trained with relevant data.

The FUTURE DIGITAL ECOSYSTEM should be built so that it accommodates not only current digital systems and technologies but emerging technologies that will also facilitate the exchange of information and results from future digital applications. The ecosystem also needs to be secure to ensure only the right people, systems and technologies have access to the right data at the right time—and only as long as they need it.

Irrespective of the level of digital maturity your company is at, each of these pillars will help to improve its position. The value that data generates from connected devices can help your business get ahead of the competition. Leveraging IoT in the supply chain, along with capabilities such as analytics or AI, enables understanding, interpretation and simulation of supply chain data so you can arrive at sustainable improvements. The results: faster, cheaper, increased efficiencies and the ability to predict future market needs via an agile and adaptive supply chain.

Digital applications for SCM today and tomorrow

The nine key digital technologies relevant for supply chains are outlined in the graphic (see Figure 3: Digital applications for SCM) below. More complete details of what they are, how each adds value to the supply chain, and their advantages and challenges can be seen at the end of the chapter and the two chapters dedicated to Advanced Analytics and AI that follow.

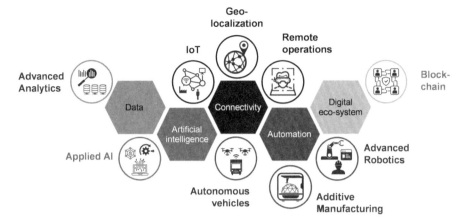

Figure 3: Digital applications for SCM

The current state of play in supply chains

The message is spreading that data is one of the most valuable assets a company can have. This is probably why there's currently significantly more interest in Advanced Analytics than in any of the other eight technologies. Companies see the advantages to be gained by scaling it across their entire supplier network. This is why there's a direct link between the Internet of Things (IoT), glocalization and Advanced Analytics, as they collect data that is the feedstuff of Advanced Analytics. Research conducted by h&z revealed that in 2020, 87% of companies we surveyed currently use, pilot or plan to use analytics. What is surprising is the level of widespread and full implementation of the nine key technologies, where only 5% claimed to have fully implemented analytics across all functions and the supply chain.

One surprising finding in our survey was that 8% of companies are making full use of autonomous vehicle technologies. However, this refers largely to warehouse or manufacturing operations where there are goods to handle or machine-to-machine interfaces for intralogistics transports.

Despite its huge potential, the use of Artificial Intelligence hasn't moved much beyond the planning stage as the technology itself is still in its early phase of development. However, as we'll see below, there will be a dramatic change to the current status quo in the next few years.

Increased speed and efficiency are the most obvious benefits

According to the h&z research study conducted in 2020, increased speed and efficiency are the two most expected benefits that will be achieved by using new technologies. Followed by transparency, which will indirectly increase efficiency by uncovering weak points within the supply chain and leading the way for their elimination. Cost reduction potentials along the supply chain are also rated high as well as improvements in collaboration. Of far less importance are revenue increases and environmental sustainability.

The year 2025: Advanced Analytics and AI will lead the way

Despite its current limited application, the use of AI will grow significantly until 2025. This and Advanced Analytics will impact all facets of supply chains and will pave the way to faster and more informed decision making that can then be actioned using the new technologies.

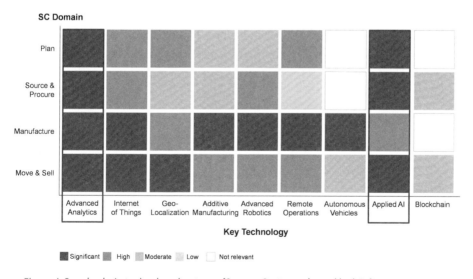

Figure 4: Supply chain technology heat map (Source: Gartner adapted by h&z)

Planners will play a different role, moving away from crystal ball thinking to using analytics and correlation-based patterns to evaluate trends based on market insights. The use of analytics and the pairing of IoT with geo-localization will play a significant role in ensuring and accelerating delivery speed and accuracy in the area of move and sell. But also technologies like autonomous driving—once passing legislation barriers—will see a rise in the years 2025–2030 according to a h&z research study.

The Author's perspective

These are exciting times in the world of supply chain management. The array of digital technologies, that are available for use now, brings with it the promise of greater speed, efficiency, and transparency, to name just the obvious benefits. That said, digital applications are still a long way from being widely used in today's supply chains. Part of the reason for this is that the supply chain is still largely seen by company leaders as a cost rather than a revenue generator, and consequently there is considerably less investment in it than in other business functions such as marketing.

But the momentum is shifting and we expect to see sustained efforts to digitally transform the supply chain. Driven by data availability and the current drive to set up data lakes, Advanced Analytics will be the first of the technologies featured here that will gain importance. This will be helped as the quality of the data generated by IoT improves. To get ready, pilot projects need to be launched in coordination and with an overall cross-functional roadmap.

A strategy ties it all together

However, the availability of these nine key digital technologies and the benefits inherent in their use is undermined unless you have a concerted strategy for why, how and where to use them. As we'll see in Chapter 4.3, a digital strategy forms the foundation for successfully managing the digital transformation process, which in turn leads to a stronger drive to implement solutions.

Think about people

Finally, let's not forget the people who are supposed to work with these technologies in a newly digitalized supply chain. Efforts to digitally transform your business are likely to fail unless your business also goes through a cultural transformation. It is the people, not technology, that are the biggest hurdle to digital transformation. Chapter 4.2 looks at this in detail.

Digital evolution along the supply chain

To understand their stage of maturity we provide companies with an evolutionary path along the different supply chain functions alongside pertinent examples.

It should be noted that the intention of the maturity measure is not that each company needs to reach the final maturity stage for each element since the underlying business case to address improvements may not be given for each step. For example, for a mid-sized company, it would be important to evaluate if a high-cost, fully automated picking and commissioning system adds value to the full system over a partly optimized system, where picking is provided in sequence but executed by humans.

We can review the digital evolution along different supply chain domains by looking at examples. The evolution ranges from pre-digital—or the traditional supply chain setup—to digital functions, where digitalization is applied to individual processes.

"We've prioritized areas where we can increase our competitiveness on a pillar-to-pillar basis rather than starting a large project with the main question 'What is digitization?'"

Thorsten Rosenberg, Executive Vice President & Head of Global Supply Chain, BSH Hausgeräte GmbH

When it comes to digital supply chains, value chains, or even ecosystems that include multiple trading partners along the value chain, we can help to create, for example, full N-Tier demand transparency.

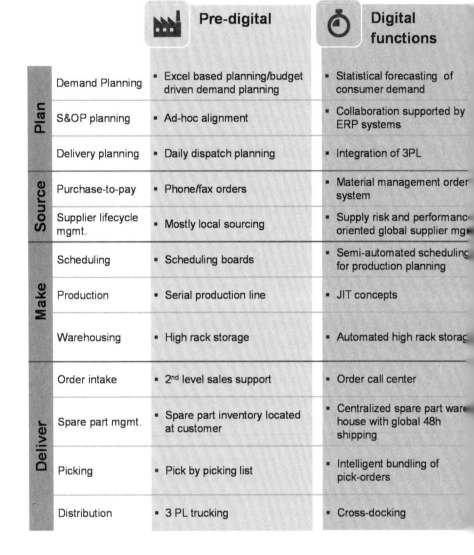

		▦ **Pre-digital**	⏱ **Digital functions**
Plan	Demand Planning	• Excel based planning/budget driven demand planning	• Statistical forecasting of consumer demand
	S&OP planning	• Ad-hoc alignment	• Collaboration supported by ERP systems
	Delivery planning	• Daily dispatch planning	• Integration of 3PL
Source	Purchase-to-pay	• Phone/fax orders	• Material management order system
	Supplier lifecycle mgmt.	• Mostly local sourcing	• Supply risk and performance oriented global supplier mgm
Make	Scheduling	• Scheduling boards	• Semi-automated scheduling for production planning
	Production	• Serial production line	• JIT concepts
	Warehousing	• High rack storage	• Automated high rack storag
Deliver	Order intake	• 2nd level sales support	• Order call center
	Spare part mgmt.	• Spare part inventory located at customer	• Centralized spare part ware house with global 48h shipping
	Picking	• Pick by picking list	• Intelligent bundling of pick-orders
	Distribution	• 3 PL trucking	• Cross-docking

Figure 5: Evolution along supply chain dimensions

Digital supply chain	Digital value chain	Digital ecosystem
Advanced Analytics for Demand Planning	Collaboration of demand	N Tier Demand Alignment through cloud services
S&OP as collaboration function supported by ERP/Data	Scenario based planning considering multiple variables	AI driven decision models to drive optimal scenarios
SC tower centrally controlling global logistics	Real-time SC flow monitoring and re-routing	Self-controlling logistics network
e-2-e integrated catalogue purchasing	Chat-bot ordering supported by purchase suggestions	Automated push supply based on forecast or IoT
360° integrated global supplier management	N-tier supplier management	B/C suppliers managed through sourcing networks
Automated scheduling optimization and heuristics	Multi level heuristics and optimization	Parts find their own schedule in flexible production stations
For- and backward forecast information and integration	Robots next to humans	Self-organizing flexible production set-ups
Chaotic storage system managed by 3PL	RFID supported storage (depending on product)	Goods to man combined with business case driven logistics concepts
Outsourced order call center	Chat bots for simple ordering tasks	Chat bots for all general ordering tasks
Preventive maintenance spare part shipping	Preventive spare part exchange under up-time contract	On-site 3D spare part printing by specialized providers
Route optimized static picking	Real-time/dynamic picking route optimization	Automated picking & packaging at human speed in a chaotic storage system
Real-time track & trace and route optimization	Automated trucking on long-haul	

The nine digital technologies in detail

ADVANCED ANALYTICS
(See Chapter 2.2 for a deep dive into Advanced Analytics)

What is it?
Advanced Analytics is what allows us to make sense of Big Data. It's an evolution of BI. Put simply, Advanced Analytics is a research and analysis tool that can help drive change and improvement in future business processes.

How does it help?
There are two types of Advanced Analytics:
- **Predictive Analytics**, as the name suggests, helps predict what might happen.
- **Prescriptive Analytics** is used to help identify the most appropriate business decisions.

Advanced Analytics is useful for analyzing events and behaviors. It does this via real-time analysis of huge data sets to identify patterns and make predictions, thereby helping people to make much more informed decisions.

In SCM, Advanced Analytics is typically used to make decisions about future events like production capacity. It can also play a role in predicting the cost of raw materials and future demand. In other words, it helps to avoid lost sales and optimize inventory. It also saves time. If an autonomous analysis process only needs the approval of a manager at the end of a process, it frees up the manager to work on other value-adding tasks.

How does it add value?
- It enables the use of **what-if analyses** to predict the impact of potential changes in corporate business strategies.
- **Data mining**: It's a far more sophisticated tool and much more effective at searching for patterns within data than traditional business intelligence methods.
- **Machine learning**: Self-learning analysis algorithms enable forecasts generation from existing data that are significantly more accurate compared to previous forecasting possibilities. It is the basis for predictive maintenance.

- **Cognitive analytics:** This is the highest level of Advanced Analytics and will greatly ease management decision making as there's no need for analysis, only approval of the outcome.

Threats & Challenges:
- Collecting, storing and structuring the large amounts of data involved.
- Data structuring: How do you aggregate all data from different sources and model a logical data structure?[3]

ARTIFICIAL INTELLIGENCE
(See Chapter 2.3 for a deep dive into AI)

What is it?
The hype about Artificial Intelligence (AI) is based on the technological advances in the field of deep learning. Think of deep learning (DL), neural networks, machine learning (ML) and AI as a set of Matryoshka dolls, where a series of diminishing, brightly colored dolls nestles snuggly within each other. If AI is the mother of all dolls, machine learning is next in line, the oldest sibling, followed by deep learning, the younger sister. So, DL is a subset of ML, which in turn is a subset of AI.

How does it help?
AI can be applied in various fields of business. Complex relationships can be uncovered, and patterns can be recognized more quickly. As far as you and your business are concerned, the focus should be on getting better results through applications that exploit special-purpose or narrowly applied AI technologies, both leading-edge and older.

How does it add value?
Applications such as AI-based decision proposals to change production batches will have a huge and disruptive impact. They are most useful to companies when they support employees in their tasks and speed up processes (cost reduction) or when they can deliver better insight (value creation).

Threats & Challenges:

- **Huge potential:** Although we're only at the beginning of what AI can potentially do it will remain one of the most prominent technological topics in the coming years.
- **The expectation gap:** The biggest challenge is to manage the significant gap in expectations between what AI can theoretically do and how it's currently used. The algorithms are based on fundamental mathematical rules that don't always adapt well to the non-deterministic, fluid environment of the real word.
- **Data bias:** The quality of the result is dependent on the quality of the data inputs.

 # INTERNET OF THINGS (IOT)

What is it?

IoT consists of objects that become "smart" through the installation of gateways. These enable them to communicate directly with other systems via the Internet. Each smart object is assigned a unique identifier that can be used to authenticate it in the network.

How does it help?

The scope of application ranges from general information supply and automatic orders to warning and emergency functions. It is crucial to distinguish between industry and for consumer use cases.

Consumer-oriented IoT is designed for individual users at home or in the office. Common examples included smart TV, connected streaming devices, home control devices, and voice-command systems used to run your home.

Industry-oriented IoT (IIoT) makes use of sensors to measure what's happening in its environment, including location, temperature, light levels, and speed of movement. RFID chips, smart devices, and mobile sensors are common examples of IoT technology used in the supply chain.

How does it add value?

- **Time saved:** Tasks can be automated.
- **Lower susceptibility to errors** and when they do occur, they are reported in real time.
- **Better decision making** due to a higher amount of data.
- **Improved efficiency** that may result in new opportunities.
- **Predictive analytics**, leads to more accurate predictions.

Threats & Challenges:

- **Data security and privacy**—if it's online it's at risk.
- **Business & IT buy in:** Your company and its suppliers have to fully commit for it to work as it should.
- **Compatibility & longevity:** Using IoT requires the deployment of hardware and software to connect devices but some of these technologies will eventually become outmoded, effectively rendering the system and its connected devices obsolete.
- **Standards:** Technology standards, which include network protocols, communication protocols.
- **Cost-value ratio:** For low cost items the initial cost of implementing an IoT system is high and may not be considered worth the investment.[4]

 BLOCKCHAIN

What is it?

Explained in simple words: *"I loan Paul €2 and five friends witness me do this. Those five friends are now the Blockchain."* It is in effect a publicly accessible database *(those five friends)* that maintains a constantly growing list of chronological transaction records (like adding links to a chain). In reality the chain is endless and never forgets because all previous transactions are saved in a ledger document that all people using the blockchain have. This is an example from the world of finance, but equally translates to supply chains.

How does it help?

Blockchain is well suited to verify the authenticity of a parcel, for example. It's a trusted, secure, fast, and cost-efficient method of completing transactions such as shipping documents, export documentation or tracking products.

How does it add value?

- **Data protection:** Protects large volumes of data with encryption and access management.
- **Easier verification** of data reference points.
- **Automatic detection of fraud** in the supply chain, payment transactions and other business processes.
- **Information flows** are anonymous, decentralized and processed faster while being more secure and reliable.
- **Clearly defined ownership structure**, low transaction fees, data transparency.
- **Cheaper payment processing** that's also considerably faster and more efficient.
- **Fail-safe data storage** with countless replications massively reduces the likelihood of failure.

Threats & Challenges:

Interoperability: The lack of standards (such as coding language, protocols, uniform regulation or transnational laws) is likely to lead to **regulation and governance**.

Integration: How can it be included in the current IT system?

Energy expenditure: It will be necessary to find a way of using it that is energy-efficient.

Storage space: A new way of storing or compressing data is crucial.

Cost efficiency: Blockchain requires a "critical mass" of nodes to work efficiently.[5]

"A lot of the talk surrounding blockchain is hype, in my opinion. In most of the cases I think this technology isn't necessary as conventional EDI standards could still do the work. But blockchain will be the most fitting technology to reduce the handling of freight documents in logistics companies. This would improve processes in large transport chains and therefore be a huge value-add."

Erik Wirsing, Vice President Global Innovation, DB Schenker

"Blockchain has the potential of becoming a true game changer for supply chain in the coming years. Within both procurement as well as supply chain there are a number of use cases that are well suited for block chain solutions. Blockchain solutions are still developing, but we begin to see use cases with e. g. global supply chain networks like Tradelens, that truly digitizes the global supply chain via blockchain technology. Blockchain in the supply chain is one of the next big things."

Jacob G. Larsen, Director of Digital Procurement, Maersk Group

AUTONOMOUS VEHICLES FOR TRANSPORT LOGISTICS AND INTRALOGISTICS

What is it?
Autonomous, or self-driving, vehicles guide themselves without human control from point A to point B. In logistics, these are already used in warehouses and on-site premises. A number of different logistics providers are planning to use autonomous vehicles for long-haul routes by 2025. The vehicles will drive in a single file, close to each other, which is known as platooning. The lead vehicle, which will have a driver in the cabin, controls the speed and direction, with each vehicle communicating with the others responding to the lead vehicle's movements.[6]

"Automatization and the automatization of trucks and vehicles for transporting goods opens new business models for logistics companies.

A driver could, for example, take his or her rest break during a platooning phase, which would reduce downtime."

Erik Wirsing, Vice President Global Innovation, DB Schenker

How does it help?
Self-driving systems perform complex tasks without human interaction. They release manpower to more value-added tasks such as warehouse operations and will change the way we transport goods in the future.

How does it add value?
- **Speed and efficiency** increase because simple transportation tasks in the warehouse can be performed by autonomous vehicles 24/7.
- **Extend available driver time for road transport** through e. g. platooning (this benefit still depends on legislation approval).
- **Greater control** and **productivity increases.**
- **Reduced error, rework, and risk rate**: The intuitive usability makes it possible for employees to receive information about the autonomous robots within a few minutes.
- **Improved Safety** in areas of high risk (for example in mining or agriculture).
- **Autonomous vehicles** in particular can lead to:
  - new jobs like "platoon pilot"
  - reduced accidents, traffic congestion, CO2 emissions, fuel consumption, travel time and transportation costs

Threats & Challenges:
- **Impact on Jobs:** Predictions say that in five years time human forklift drivers will no longer be required.
- **Cyber Security:** Systems that aren't highly secure will be open to attack by hackers and cyber terrorists.
- **Malfunctions:** An unexpected glitch that causes a self-driving machine to act unpredictably or stop altogether may lead to a production outage in an assembly line.
- **Insurance:** Who is responsible when two self-driving vehicles have an accident? Who pays?[7]

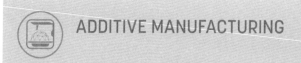

ADDITIVE MANUFACTURING

What is it?

Additive manufacturing is used to create objects by adding volume layer by layer. Additive manufacturing is used for rapid prototyping, where a prototype for conducting functional or user tests can be built in a very short time.

Three common examples:

- **Fused deposition modeling** (FDM) is used to fabricate thermoplastic objects. FDM is widely used in 3D printers.
- **Selective laser sintering** (SLS) is a powder bed technique that merges material particles layer by layer with a focused laser.
- **Stereolithography** (SL) is a method to generate objects from liquid polymers through a polymerization process that is triggered by light. It is possible to build extremely precise parts.

How does it help?

With additive manufacturing, it's possible to join materials to create and shape parts with high precision from a wide range of materials on demand and at a low cost. Additive manufacturing is particularly suited to the engineering of spare parts and the page assembly of difficult, weight-critical parts.

How does it add value?

- **Produce a greater range of shapes** that were not previously feasible within reasonable time limits and at realistic costs.
- **Faster production** and the ability to make parts overnight increases efficiency and flexibility.
- **Customization** means production can be more customer focused.
- Form follows function so with **fewer production restrictions** better, tailor-made components can be created.
- A **range of different materials can be used** in comparison to traditional manufacturing techniques.

Threats & Challenges:

- **Consistent quality:** Ensuring each 3D printed part is equal.
- **Political regulations:** Copyright and the liability for damages are questions that have to be answered.
- **Space:** It currently requires a lot of space to house additive manufacturing equipment.
- **Mass production:** It isn't suited to serial production.
- **Rework:** This has to be minimized as currently the need to re-work parts happens too frequently.
- **Process duration:** Often it takes more time to build parts with additive manufacturing technologies than with subtractive methods.[8]

 ## GEO-LOCALIZATION

What is it?

Geo-localization is technology that uses wireless detection, via GPS-, GSM- and Galileo-based positioning and sensors, to identify or estimate the real-world geographic location of remote devices. The most commonly used method in the supply chain is radio frequency (RF) location.

How does it help?

Geo-localization enables the continuous, real-time tracking and tracing of objects so it has clear uses along the supply chain, with the most obvious being the tracking of shipments between two facilities. It also has applications in risk management where it's used to identify, assess and mitigate risks based on geo-localized details.

"Geolocating and geofencing have enabled our customers to see exactly where each trailer is at any given moment. The dispositioning tool sends an immediate message to our customers about any delays or malfunctions. It means we can react flexibly and immediately to unforeseen events."

Hartwig Meinen, Managing Director Logistics,
Elflein Spedition & Transport GmbH

How does it add value?

- Whether it's used for B2B or B2C, geo-localization adds considerable **transparency** about the whereabouts of goods that are being sent or received. On the B2B side, this means it's easier to **plan production**, especially production downtimes.
- **Processes can be optimized** when you know exactly where the item you need is located.
- **Decreases the risk of error and mishandling.**
- Geo-localization also helps to **manage and lower your energy costs.**

Threats & Challenges:

- **Political regulations:** Privacy regulations regarding tracking stops.
- **Infrastructure:** There is no one-size-fits-all technology solution possible for all the potential uses of geo-localization so the current infrastructure needs to adapt and evolve to allow it to be used more widely.
- **Customer focus:** The use of connected devices paves the way for highly individualized offerings to people with specific needs.
- **Indoor location:** It remains challenging to locate parcels and goods in production facilities. However, new technologies are being developed for this.[9]

 ## REMOTE OPERATIONS

What is it?
Remote operations refer to the operation of a system or machine at a distance. This is enabled by using augmented and virtual reality and virtual tele-presence solutions that eliminate the need for people to be on-site.

How does it help?
Remote operations provide expertise, skills, and technology capabilities that customers may not have at the actual production site or site of operations.

How does it add value?

- **Speed and efficiency** (and therefore productivity) are improved because it's not necessary to add travel times to tasks, leaving operators to focus on other value-added tasks.
- Advanced wearables **open up new possibilities** for augmented reality.
- **Hands-free operations** can drive higher productivity.
- Remote expert applications can provide transformation capabilities.
- Augmented reality can be used to **train new employees** without the involvement of a third party.[10]

Threats & Challenges:

- **Isolation and information:** Never underestimate the value of face-to-face communication. Remote working can mean people lose contact with colleagues and the quality of communication may decrease, which could actually lead to an increased workload. There is also the real risk that remote employees can feel a sense of isolation.
- **Area-wide use:** Augmented and virtual reality in particular are most efficient when both suppliers and customers use them.

 ADVANCED ROBOTICS

What is it?

Advanced robotics refers to programmed machines that can interact with the real world through the use of sensors, such as touch, ultrasonic, or light. The defining characteristic of advanced robotics is decentralized intelligence that allows devices and equipment to make decisions and take actions autonomously, without human intervention. Compared to conventional robots, advanced robots have superior perception, integrability, adaptability, and mobility.[11]

The next generation of robot will be light, flexible, easy to program, affordable and able to interact with humans.

How does it help?

In the supply chain, advanced robotics has clear applications in packaging, production, and process automatization. The technology also lies at the heart of automated guided vehicles.

How does it add value?

- **Speed and efficiency (productivity)**: Routine tasks no longer need to be done by people but by a robot, leaving people more time for value-adding activities.
- **Quality:** Advanced robots can outperform human workers on some tasks, such as assembly, delivering greater reliability and precision.
- **Agility:** The technology is easily configured to new production systems to meet the rising demand for more product variations, customized products, and product redesigns.
- **Decreasing prices:** The cost of advanced robotics is going down as the prices for sensors and computing power decrease, and software increasingly replaces hardware as the primary driver of functionality.
- **Safety:** Advanced robots can perform tasks that are dangerous or physically demanding for human workers.

Threats & Challenges:

- **Factory-of-the-future:** These self-controlled facilities will operate with as little human interaction as possible and will be readily adjustable to new customer needs.
- **Acquiring costs:** The cost of advanced robotics will gradually reduce so its use will become more widespread.[12]

Chapter 2.2
Advanced Analytics: Powerful and indispensable
Tony Zscheye
How to successfully facilitate the application of
Advanced Analytics in your organization

Introduction

Do you know how much 33 zettabytes are? 33 zettabytes are approximately equivalent to the total amount of digital data generated worldwide in 2018. In common units it is 33 billion terabytes. That doesn't just sound like a lot—if viewed in the right context, it is a lot. In 2010 only around 1.2 zettabytes of data were generated. Current predictions estimate that the total volume of data generated annually will more than quintuple by 2025. This means that in 2025, around 175 zettabytes will be generated. This large quantity of data will open the way to great possibilities.

When we talk about Big Data, the term is often understood mainly in terms of data quantity. This understanding, however, is far too limited. Based on a recently conducted study, the successful utilization of digital applications in the supply chain is dependent on the appropriate and context-specific usage of data. Word is spreading that data is one of the most valuable assets a company can have. This is probably why we've been seeing significantly more interest in Advanced Analytics than in any of the other eight technologies that were the focus of this recent study.

In this chapter we dive into the application of Advanced Analytics in general and more specifically in regard to supply chain management. We also explore the challenges and key enablers for its successful application within projects and organizations. A number of examples will be used to illustrate how this cutting-edge technology is being put to use.[1]

What is Big Data actually? What is Advanced Analytics?

Surely, you've already heard of Big Data and Advanced Analytics. You probably know that there are many different definitions of the two terms, both individually and combined. How would you describe them? Can the people who you discuss this topic with actually explain what they are? In the following, we are going to give you our detailed understanding and the definitions of the terms Big Data and Advanced Analytics.[2]

Big Data

One reason for the many different definitions of Big Data lies in the general term "big." It normally leads to a comprehension of something merely in terms of quantification. The term "big," however, also refers to the complexity and significance of the respective data. In our understanding, Big Data refers to a massive volume of both structured and unstructured data that is complex and extremely difficult to process using traditional databases and software techniques. Still, it is important to characterize Big Data even further. There are several so-called Multi-V models like the 4-V model by IBM or the 3-V model by Gartner which try to characterize Big Data in a more differentiated approach. We are going to take a look at the 5-V model according to Assunçaoã et al. (2014) or Addo-Tenkorang, R., Helo, P.T. (2016) which is the most comprehensive and thus best describes the complex concept of Big Data in its complete extent and as well as its impact. The 5-V model consists of the following five characteristics: Variety (data types), Velocity (data production and processing speed), Volume (data size), Veracity (data reliability and trust) and Value.
In more detail:

1. Variety

   Refers to the spectrum of potential input data such as regular internal sources, historical data, machine data, or completely new data like current weather conditions and through to entirely new data sources such as social media content and even video content.

2. Volume

   Refers to the quantity of data, with a special focus on storage capabilities as a limiting factor. For example, it is estimated that every day, 2.3 trillion gigabytes of data are produced.

3. Velocity

   Refers to the ever-increasing need for rapid data processing. If batch processing was sufficient in the past (time intervals, e.g. always updating the previous day's data overnight), the demands concerning processing speed become much higher. The subsequent steps are near-time (smaller time intervals), real-time (within milliseconds) and data streaming (instant analysis of data flows).

4. Veracity

   Refers to the importance of data quality and the level of trust in regard to the reliability of individual data sources.

5. Value

   Refers to the process of identifying important, thus far unexploited insights through Big Data, which can then be used to support the decision-making process.

As a basic model, the 5-V model helps to create a comprehensible and traceable connection between the data. The analysis/categorization allows the data to be perfectly adjusted for the respective purpose. In this context Big Data must be seen as a business model. In order to achieve the last point in this model, "Value," the previous points must be contemplated. It also tries to capture and minimize the complexity that Big Data possesses.[3]

Advanced Analytics

Advanced Analytics describes the far more important topic for you. Applied correctly, significant added value for companies can be achieved in many ways.

Advanced Analytics is the next step in data analysis beyond business Intelligence (BI). It is the (semi-)autonomous analysis of data in order to gain knowledge, predict outcomes and develop decision proposals. It uses techniques such as data/text mining, machine learning, pattern matching, forecasting, visualization, semantic analysis, sentiment analysis, network and cluster analysis, multivariate statistics, graph analysis, simulation, complex event processing and neural networks.

To put it simply, Advanced Analytics can help to drive change and improvement in future business processes. More precisely, it is the means of examining Big Data using sophisticated techniques and tools, typically beyond those of traditional BI. It is used to uncover deeper insights, make predictions, or generate recommendations and improve business planning.

The term Advanced Analytics spans various development stages that describe the maturity level regarding output/input data as well as the added value. In this way, we distinguish between three major stages in both directions. Horizontally, we distinguish between "information," "knowledge," which is information put into context, and "wisdom," which describes the derivation of decisions or decision proposals based on gained knowledge. To arrange all four maturity levels into this framework, we must also take time as a factor into account. Where Descriptive Analytics deals with analysis of the past, Diagnostic Analytics deals with the analysis of the near

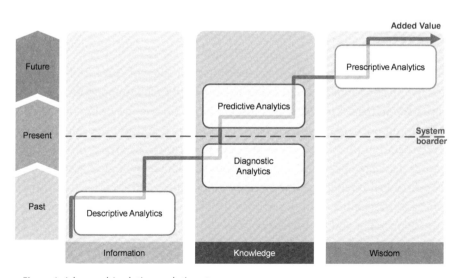

Figure 6: Advanced Analytics evolution steps

past up to the present. Predictive Analytics already places findings into the near future, whereas Prescriptive Analytics makes recommendations for the future. The system boarder describes a significant change within internal systems of a company. It is necessary to adapt these systems in order to be able to make the step towards Advanced Analytics.

As of today, Advanced Analytics begins with Predictive Analytics and peaks in Prescriptive Analytics because in these two stages at least semi-autonomous usage and evaluation of data takes place. Therefore, we would like to dive deeper into these two forms of Advanced Analytics.[4]

Predictive Analytics

Predictive Analytics incorporates various recognition and analyzing methods such as data mining or machine learning in order to identify trends and patterns of behavior that can be derived and predicted based on a data set. The overall goal is to make cross-functional predictions within shorter time periods (e.g. daily instead of monthly) to generate new business-relevant knowledge. For example, in business, Predictive Analytics is used to analyze transactional data and identify business risks and opportunities at an early stage. Recent observations show that in Predictive Analytics applications the trend is moving towards increased user-friendliness and the ability to create faster and shorter analyses.[5]

Prescriptive Analytics

Prescriptive Analytics is the latest development stage of Advanced Analytics. The technological progress lies in automated recommendations. They are made in regard to future actions, are based on analysis of the predicted future and use generated knowledge to visualize a decision-tree containing every decision possibility. To be precise, Prescriptive Analytics utilizes the results generated prior and applies various further technological approaches like Artificial Intelligence, optimization algorithms and expert systems in a probabilistic context in order to provide adaptive, automated, constrained, time-dependent and optimal decisions.

It must be distinguished between two fundamentally different outcomes, depending on the necessity of human interaction: decision support and decision automation. While the former requires approval or rejection by a human, the latter is automatically executed. Thus, in giving decision support the algorithm undergoes a learning process by factoring in the human's decision for its next suggestion. With decision automation, parameters must be set differently if a different outcome is desired.

The basis for this is achieved through various methods such as pattern matching or multivariate statistics (to name just two). Apart from that, it needs to be mentioned that Predictive Analytics is the steppingstone for Prescriptive Analytics, seeing as it uses the former model's outcomes. Therefore, the result is highly dependent on the effectiveness of the underlying and developed model.

Apart from just helping you to stay up to date and regularly adapting your systems, Advanced Analytics offers many essential advantages with great business impact. Currently a lot of use cases for Advanced Analytics are found in SCM. This is because Advanced Analytics is especially beneficial to the very nature of SCM, which covers the entire value chain and thus includes various data sources such as external suppliers or customer data. This creates excellent implementation conditions because there are fewer initial barriers.[6]

A detailed look at the advantages of Predictive and Prescriptive Analytics as well as validations on the basis of case studies will be covered later in this chapter.

Three Key Enablers build the Foundation for Successful Implementation and Utilization

What exactly is needed to enable the effective and efficient use of Advanced Analytics? There are three key enablers that are necessary to successfully utilize Advanced Analytics within a project or across an entire organization: data, methods and people (see Figure 7).

Data: The lifeblood of Advanced Analytics

The total amount of existing data is rising over the years. However, the fact that the number and variability of publicly and privately available data sources are constantly increasing, is much more important (see Chapter 3.2

Figure 7: Key enabler building blocks Data, Methods and People

on Supply Chain Planning for detailed information). Four types of data need to be differentiated:

- Structured data: Organized into a predefined depository like a database. A distinctive feature is the discrete nature of structured data which allows for a retrieval of the contained data information (singular or combinations of data).
- Semi-structured data: Not organized in a formatted repository, but contains related information e.g. in form of metadata tagging that allows for easier access to in order to process and analyze the data.
- Unstructured data: Various different forms of data which do not fit either into databases nor contain a related, specialized form of data structure like metadata tagging.
- Mixed data: Not clearly assignable and may contain a mixture of all three data types mentioned above.

Structured, semi-structured and unstructured data can be understood as different levels, where structured data can be processed best and unstructured data can be processed the least effectively.

Data and software are usually mentioned together and go hand in hand. However, in this respect a sequential and iterative process is recommended. This means that it is important to evaluate the compatibility of given data with the software and to make necessary adjustments on both sides in order to ensure perfect alignment.

Data lakes are a key enabler of Advanced Analytics as they consist of data from numerous different sources, in the same way a natural lake has multiple streams leading in and out. A data lake can have multiple databases and documents of different formats from different sources. Data can be accessed via an Application Programming Interface (API) and then structured to make it utilizable before loading it into a database. Data lakes are a viable solution when different departments need to access data. Here, costs are a key decision factor. In general, the most flexible and scalable databases are also the most expensive, as they are often charged on a pay-per-use basis. If the data volumes are high, the costs rise proportionally. According to our experts Elena Michel and Johannes Häussler, real-time data, for example, is more expensive because it requires a great deal of effort to process.

Adidas provides a practical example. In creating a unified knowledge database, Adidas managed to present business an- alytics, financial and historical sales data, as well as web analytics data together. The various data flows were automatically processed by a software solution and fed into the data lake. This lake contains ad-hoc issues, commercial activations, levels of discount, newsletter send outs, etc. Based on this data, events were matched to actual sales. This enabled Adidas to generate a forecast by comparing the forecast day with past days in terms of planned activities, e. g. discount, newsletters, public holidays ahead, and thus predict the expected volume of sales.[7]

It is crucial to select the appropriate software by taking the data (made) available into close consideration. The challenge is to choose the right tools in a rapidly growing and fast-moving world. The choice of software depends on how it's going to be used. It is generally recommended to use technology that is already being used within the organization or by the client's unique technology landscape and to avoid system breaks. Additionally, an adequate implementation strategy is necessary to ensure the full and efficient exploitation of the steps previously performed. To simplify and harmonize the terms in the following section, we decided to refer to the data scientists as service providers and to refer to the department that is looking to use these services (Advanced Analytics) as a customer.

The primary goal is to take over non-complex and routine tasks. The model shouldn't be a black box, but instead be transparent and easy to understand. Otherwise it will likely be met with resistance from users. The results should be comprehensible for specialized departments and also be easy to explain to stakeholders.

After spending so much time talking solely about data, it is extremely necessary to acknowledge that data in itself cannot lead you and your company to success. As mentioned before, it is very important to be aware of the most suitable methods for fitting your data into the bigger picture.

Methods: What should be done and why should it be done

There's little point in having a specific tool if you don't know what it can be used for and how it should be used. It's the same with Advanced Analytics—there should be a clear identification of a meaningful business case before any decisions are made about using it. It should also be clear what should be done and why it should be done. Therefore, it makes sense to do

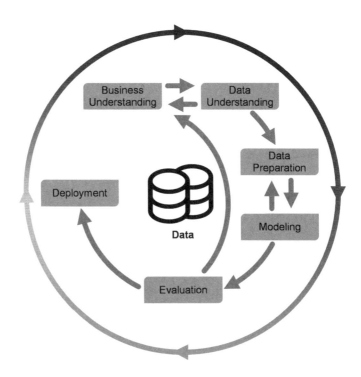

Figure 8: Cross Industry Standard Process for Data Mining (CRISP-DM)[8]

a proof of concept first, instead of tediously trying to create a complete, running system right from the beginning. Cut the proof of concept into manageable pieces, always in regard to a business case. Then ask yourself: What exactly is the benefit? Without being able to present a solid business case, it's highly unlikely that budget will be allocated to the project. Each possible use case should be assessed in order to fully recognize the savings potential.

Having a structured approach can facilitate the implementation of Advanced Analytics and help to achieve strived-for benefits. One of the most implemented processes is the CRISP-DM (CRoss-Industry Standard Process for Data Mining) model. The process is made up of six phases, as shown in Figure 8. It's important to note that the phases shouldn't necessarily be seen as strictly consecutive steps. Quite often, switching back and forth between phases is required.

Phase 1: "Business Understanding" begins with the definition of goals and requirements. The purpose is to separate those tasks with the greatest potential from the total sum of various tasks to be completed. In addition, a rough idea of how to approach the tasks should be developed.

Phase 2: "Data Understanding" involves gathering data or checking the availability of data. This helps determine possible problems regarding data quality.

Phase 3: "Data Preparation" involves construction of the final data set for modeling.

Phase 4: "Modeling" is the application of suitable data mining methods.

Phase 5: "Evaluation" of models to select that which best meets the requirements. This is where there needs to be a thorough comparison of the task and data in question. If the data turns out not to be suitable, re-assessing phase 1 may be necessary.

Phase 6: "Deployment"—This is where results are prepared and presented. If required: integration of the model into the customer's decision-making procedure. Data preparation should not be underestimated. Often, this is one of the most time-consuming steps in data mining and Advanced Analytics projects.

As the technology advances over time, so do the models. The evolution of the CRISP framework is known as ASUM-DM. There are two major differences we want to highlight.

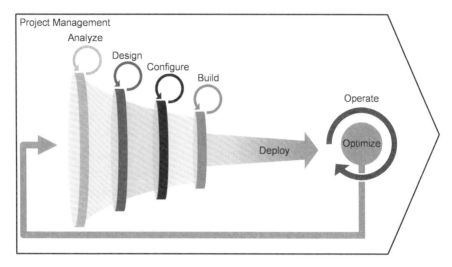

Figure 9: Analytics Solutions Unified Method for Data Mining (ASUM-DM)

The CRISP steps "Business Understanding," "Data Understanding," "Data Preparation," "Modeling and Evaluation" are more abstractly represented by "Analyze," "Design," "Configure" and "Build." This is because there are also data mining projects that do not require steps defined in the CRISP model. For example, this is the case if data is already available in the correct format and in suitable quality. The CRISP step "Data Preparation" is then obsolete.

The ASUM model contains the same "Deployment" step as the CRISP model but is followed by "Operating and Optimizing." Nowadays, this often translates to additional costs and effort, e. g. development and maintenance of an infrastructure for the analysis of large data streams.

But not everything about the new model is better. Johannes Häussler, Data Scientist at VIDATICS GmbH, also sees potential for improvement at ASUM-DM:

"It is a pity that ASUM has no explicit step for the evaluation. Even though the CRISP model is relatively old, it is still in use today. Nevertheless, the ASUM model is more suitable for today's data mining/analytics projects."

Johannes Häussler, Data Scientist, VIDATICS GmbH

Even though technology is advancing at a rapid pace and research is celebrating one milestone after another, there is one more major hurdle for industrial companies to overcome in order to unlock the full potential of AA. Employees need to be involved. Even the best methods are useless if employees don't incorporate them.

People: Any amount of data is worthless if you don't have employees who know how to make use of it

As with any process of transformation, empowering and enabling your employees to understand and use analytics is crucial for changes to be accepted. Employees need to understand, through appropriate training, what needs to be done and how it should be done. Thus, a thorough understanding of the possibilities, both for the company and themselves, is required. It is also necessary to understand how analytics data can be used to improve business and make life easier. The decision about the use of Advanced Analytics will most likely be made by the leadership, though often without enough consideration of the implications further down the hierarchy. The challenges and opportunities involved are outlined and explained in detail in Chapter 4.2 on Cultural Transformation.

The need to adapt to skill sets, which will be required through the continuous increase of Big Data and Advanced Analytics usage, is unavoidable. Based on current literature, there are eight skill sets in particular, which will become highly important: Business Impact, Project Management, Database Management, Analytics, Coding, Systems Management, Distributed Computing and Cloud Architecture. Job requirements will change, jobs will shift, and new jobs will appear. We will deal with this topic extensively in Chapter 4.1 on Future Roles.[9]

The availability of skilled analytics operatives and data scientists is relatively low, according to Elena Michel, Manager Data Analytics at rpc company. Therefore, it makes sense to support and educate internal employees while also hiring temporary external support.

Finding the right data scientist for an Advanced Analytics project or for generally implementing AA in your company is crucial. It is important for the data scientist to understand where the data is coming from and what can be achieved by applying it. The data scientist should be knowledgeable about building data products. Machine learning, statistics and probability science should all be part of the data scientist's set of skills. The use of scientific methods and the ability to prepare and perform experiments should also be part of the skill set. Also, the data scientist needs to understand and be able to interpret the data, at least up to a certain degree.[10]

There are three types of work in Advanced Analytics projects: building visuals and dashboards, building databases and modeling data. Due to the different nature of these important tasks, as a data scientist you cannot work alone, and instead, usually need to rely on the help of a team of individuals specialized in each of the different areas. Having sparring partners for creative problem-solving also has obvious benefits. The idea here is that it is important for data scientists to be able to quickly exchange information concerning current problems in order to solve them. Because this is another essential advantage, data scientists (as of today) neither focus on nor are limited to specific industries or analysis methods. It is important to recognize that a data scientist is not an expert in all areas, as they highly differ in their expertise.

The question arises, does it make sense to permanently integrate data scientists into the organization or rather to employ them as and when they're needed? This largely depends on what is currently being done with the data rather than on the company's size. Fully employing data scientists could make as much sense for a small start-up as it does for a mid-size company. If you are unsure about hiring a data scientist as a full-time employee, it makes sense to gain experience with pilot cases, in which a data scientist is temporarily integrated into a project team and their impact is afterwards evaluated.

Finally, it is important to manage expectations about what can and cannot be done with Advanced Analytics. It must be made clear that for some situations, no data analytics models can be applied. This would be the case for one-off or seldomly occurring events, for which no historical data is available. For example, it's very hard to design models for the effects of Brexit, Dr Hausmann says.

Summary key enablers

Although the three key enablers were described consecutively, it is essential that these enablers are approached and worked with simultaneously. It's a learning curve for all participants. People become familiarized with these new methods and data sources and gradually increase their knowledge and skills in dealing with them. At the same time, the methods are also gradually being validated or falsified and then replaced. The same applies to the data sources.

It should be noted that ultimately, only vertical integration across all three key factors will lead to a gradual improvement in results. If one of the three factors—data, method, people—is much more developed than the other factors, an imbalance can occur, which puts the entire project or organization in a challenging position. The preferred way should be to continuously improve in all three areas.

Fields of Application of Advanced Analytics in SCM

What better than to explain and validate the previously explained by means of an example? Therefore, we would like to present two use cases to highlight the advantages.

Case study: Optimized Logistics—ORION program at UPS

UPS delivery drivers make approximately 100 delivery stops per day. More than 4 billion items are shipped throughout a year in almost 100,000 vehicles. UPS has used Advanced Analytics in a number of ways to improve the efficiency of its business, most notably for fleet optimization as part of its ORION program.

ORION uses on-truck telematics and advanced algorithms to reduce engine idle time, predict maintenance, and to determine the most efficient routes for pick-ups and deliveries. Some of the attributes it uses are start time, delivery time, pick-up windows, traffic, and special customer needs. This data is then used by an online map to compute trip lengths along the most cost-effective routes. All vehicles have been equipped with GPS trackers and vehicle sensors. By deploying these, together with the handheld mobile device used by each driver, UPS is able to track data about vehicle routes and the length of time that each vehicle remained stationary.

The ORION program was implemented on 55,000 routes in North America and as a result, trip distances were reduced by roughly 160 million kilometers per year. This translates to a net decrease in fuel consumption of almost 38 million liters annually and a correlating reduction of approximately 100,000 metric tons of carbon dioxide.

As the UPS use case shows, Advanced Analytics can be a great tool to optimize your profits.

In addition to the cost reduction described in the use case, there are further advantages to Advanced Analytics. These will briefly be explained in the next section.

General advantages

TRANSPARENCY. Advanced Analytics helps to improve transparency because it can be used to merge internal and external information, leading to a better picture of what's going on.

COLLABORATION. Advanced Analytics helps to improve the communication of key activities between different partners in the supply chain.

SUSTAINABILITY. Advanced Analytics is very useful for improving detection of blind spots in your business, highlighting risk and flagging opportunities that may otherwise have remained undetected.

IMPROVED DECISION MAKING. Whether it's a decision linked to a business strategy, or a very specific decision relating to a specific SCM operating model, Advanced Analytics can help provide insights to make these decisions easier.

EFFICIENCY. Processes can be optimized by gaining a better understanding of current inefficiencies. It becomes easier to achieve operational effectiveness in supply chain processes.

AGILITY. Because of the availability of real-time data and information and their role in decision making when used in Predictive and Prescriptive Analytics, the utilization of Advanced Analytics leads to improved response times regarding changes.

SCALABILITY. Databases can be enlarged by combining information from traditional supply chain management systems, ERP systems and other applications that are not connected. Statistical methods can then be applied to the entire, single database, which is accessible to a larger user base and has better usability.

> "Current technologies like AI and Big Data are important for logistics since we are dealing with huge amounts of data from many different customers. Data processing will be particularly important in logistics of the future. Needless to say, they are important technologies which will facilitate many processes."
>
> Erik Wirsing, Vice President Global Innovation, DB Schenker

We recently presented one out of hundreds of case studies in order to convey a first impression, a kind of teaser, of how powerful Advanced Analytics is. In the further course of the book, more case studies, which also (partly) refer to Advanced Analytics will be shown to prove that Advanced Analytics will lead the way in the future. Nevertheless, it should be stated that implementing Advanced Analytics is not a trivial task and that there will be challenges along the way.

Challenges

There are definite challenges when it comes to using Advanced Analytics. In terms of people as a factor, the shortage of qualified employees is particularly noticeable in the data scientist field, due to the novelty of this area and the high demand across all industries. According to our survey of supply chain experts, 18% of companies want to fully implement Advanced Analytics. In addition, 65% of respondents said they plan to use Advanced Analytics selectively. After planning Advanced Analytics projects in supply chain management, the organizations face a conflict between a small supply of qualified employees and an increasing demand for these. This is part of a bigger issue linked to digital transformation within the supply chain, specifically corporate culture and people transformation, a topic that will be discussed in detail in Chapter 4.2 and 4.3.

Usually, tools to support this process exist. Though in general, the next steps and further implications are not known. The problem is made even greater by lack of expertise in this area and by the fact that the few available data scientists are in high demand. When it comes to data, problems arise not because of what's available but because of how it's shared.

All departments within a company generate data, but we find that sometimes there's reluctance to share it between departments. Think of data as pieces of a puzzle—you can't see the whole picture until all the pieces are brought together. In the same way, data from one department may need to be enriched with data sets from other departments in order to attain a full understanding of what's going on. Hence, data needs to be shared within the company.

It can also take a very long time until data is received and processed—60–80% of a data scientist's time is consumed by data preparation, data treatment and data understanding. Creating value from Big Data is made difficult by the fact that very few companies have predefined processes to analyze and evaluate it. Outdated IT systems can also become a hurdle.

Data security and data privacy can become contradicting goals when using Advanced Analytics methods (using as much data as possible needs to be weighed against data security and data privacy). This should always be considered carefully. Depending on the geographic location, legal restrictions may also be a limiting factor to its use.

Roadmap to successful implementation of Advanced Analytics

 Careful planning is the name of the game when it comes to successfully completing an Advanced Analytics project. Figure 5 shows one approach. It includes the three key enablers.

It is always very important to have a structured approach, such as defined in the ASUM processes. It is also very important for the client and the team to have common goals, based on a clear understanding of the client's requirements and expectations. Also, managing the client's expectations (e.g. if expectations are unrealistic) is crucial. Before beginning with analysis, you should take the time to gain deep understanding of a high-quality database.

Always ensure that there are knowledgeable and experienced data scientists available to work on the project. They require a clear understanding of

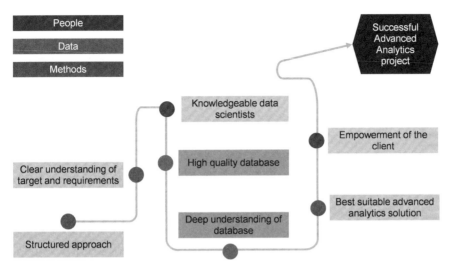

Figure 10: Roadmap to successful Advanced Analytics implementation

the business case behind the project, granted a business case exists. A good data scientist may provide ideas for applications that others might not have thought of.

The next step is to fully understand the current processes and tools that are being used around the database. Always use up-to-date technology and software and apply the most suitable Advanced Analytics solution to each individual case.

Finally, it is very important to empower your staff. They will be working with the tool and will have a clear sense of what needs to be done and how the results can be used in a meaningful way.

Conclusion

Big Data, and especially Advanced Analytics, offers tremendous possibilities for improving nearly every step of the supply chain. But it's not something that happens overnight. It requires an intensive engagement with the emerging issue. This includes the right preparation in terms of knowledge build-up, knowledge transfer, availability of resources and a certain amount of investment power and willingness.

The interaction between data, methods and people is the key to success. It is fundamentally important to understand that each part of this triangle operates in harmony with the others. Even if internal discussions concerning the availability of capabilities, especially knowledge, arise, you should start with a pilot case. In this still relatively open and unexplored field, it is necessary to take the first steps now and to not wait for best practices to be defined. Those who don't follow and try out now will be left behind by the market. You should not forget that the supply chain already provides a lot of data, making it predestined for Advanced Analytics. In this respect, the first measured results are already available, even though only a few companies are successfully using Advanced Analytics as a supply chain management tool. They report that it helps with gaining visibility on expenditure, identifying trends in cost and performance, process control, inventory monitoring, production optimization and process improvement efforts to only name a few. So, what are you waiting for?

Chapter 2.3
Artificial Intelligence:
Supply Chains will never be the same
Matthias Dicke

Introduction

"Within the past few years, important advances have occurred in many separate areas of Artificial Intelligence, computer science, and microelectronics. [...] Advances in machine vision, speech, and machine understanding of natural language provide easy ways for humans to interact with computers. [...] We stand at the threshold of a new generation of computing technology having unprecedented capabilities [...]. For example, instead of fielding simple guided missiles or remotely piloted vehicles, we might launch completely autonomous land, sea, and air vehicles capable of complex, far-ranging reconnaissance and attack missions."[1]

This chilling quote comes from the 1983 US Government-supported Defense Advanced Research Projects Agency's (DARPA) Strategic Computing Initiative (SCI). It provided more than US$1bn worth of funding over a ten-year period for research and development into machine intelligence, including chip design and manufacture, computer architecture and Artificial Intelligence software. In effect, it signaled a new arms race, a race to be the predominant force in Artificial Intelligence (AI), especially its military applications. The program was shut down in 1987 because it failed to meet its goal of high-level machine intelligence because, according to the head of the initiative, AI was not "the next wave."[2]

The state of AI looks very different today. It's now gone way beyond being "the next wave" and is more of a tsunami, ready to engulf us all in the changes it will bring to the way we work and how we live our lives. For these reasons, this seems like a good time to review the current hype about AI and, more specifically, to take a deeper look at its implications for supply chain management.

AI, ML, DL: What does it all mean?

The topic of AI is complex, so we'll begin with some jargon-busting explanations and clarifications.

In Chapter 2.1, it was suggested that AI, machine learning (ML) and deep learning (DL) can be likened to a set of Matryoshka dolls, where each brightly colored figure nestles snuggly within its larger sister. To put it simply, DL is a subset of ML, which in turn is a subset of AI.

AI itself is a term for any computer program that does something smart. It's capable of more than machine learning. More precisely, AI is human intelligence performed by machines or as a system that mimics and at some point, will surpass human thinking. Over time, five abilities have been defined that are considered essential for AI: the ability to perceive, understand, learn, problem solve, and to reason.[3]

The recent hype about AI has been fueled by progress in deep learning and advances in machine learning. Deep learning is characterized by many layers where each layer analyzes a different aspect of the data, so it gets its name from this high number of layers. DL algorithms are very good at perceiving patterns. For example, after seeing many photographs of the human face it can automatically extract high-level features from data such as the fact that eyes and ears are essential features.[4]

Machine learning: three types

MACHINE LEARNING can be split into three different types: supervised ML, unsupervised ML and reinforced ML.

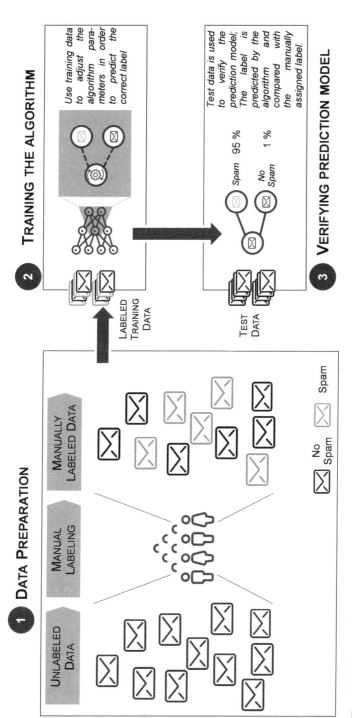

Figure 11: Supervised Machine Learning

SUPERVISED ML helps to automate repetitive tasks but needs manually pre-assigned labels to enable it to learn. It is data driven and especially suitable for tasks related to actions. Examples of how it is used include spam filters, image recognition, voice pattern recognition, next best action, churn rate prediction (for employees and customers), and predictive maintenance. Figure 11 shows how it is used for filtering spam. Mail needs to be labeled manually (for example, by moving certain emails to the spam folder), before an algorithm identifies which characteristics the spam mails have in common. It can then adjust its model to identify whether a mail is spam or not. After adjusting its parameters, the supervised ML algorithm tests itself by using spam mail and regular mail to assess its own predictions.[5]

By contrast, UNSUPERVISED ML doesn't need any labeling. It can organize data in three ways, depending on the problem.[6]

The first is **clustering.** Given data points relating to height and weight for people, it would not be too difficult to roughly gather these into male (higher weight and height) and female (lower weight and height). So unsupervised machine learning looks for data points that are similar to each other and puts them into clusters. Figure 12 illustrates how it's used for facial recognition. After being trained with thousands of pictures it can distinguish between images that show faces and those that don't. The algorithm identifies which characteristics are most appropriate for identifying faces. However, these clusters still need a human operative to identify and name them.

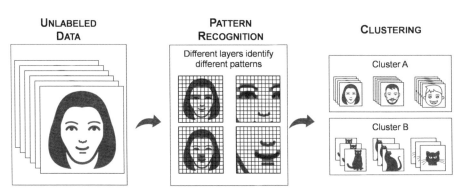

Figure 12: Unsupervised Machine Learning for clustering

The second way unsupervised ML organizes data is **anomaly detection.** Think of a production process that involves noise and temperature. Unusual readings in either could be indicators of something that isn't quite right. Even if loud noises or high temperatures are in themselves nothing to cause alarm, a combination of them might indicate a problem. Unsupervised ML is used to give alerts when such problem indicators are detected. However, the algorithm isn't given a definition of what is abnormal beforehand.

The third way in which unsupervised ML distinguishes data points is **association**, where certain features of a data set are associated with others. An example of this is segmenting customers based on social demographic data or behavior. Another example comes from online shopping, where the contents of your shopping cart is analyzed to see which goods are often bought together.

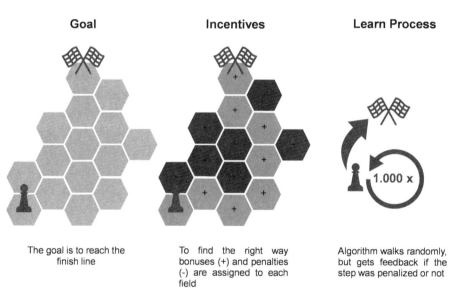

Goal	Incentives	Learn Process
The goal is to reach the finish line	To find the right way bonuses (+) and penalties (-) are assigned to each field	Algorithm walks randomly, but gets feedback if the step was penalized or not

Figure 13: Reinforced Machine Learning

REINFORCED ML, the third type of machine learning, is based on learning by trial and error. It's especially useful in cases where programs or robots need to make several decisions. Think of being taught to play a game such as chess, where there is a series of moves that will take you to the end goal of winning the game. Your teacher will give you feedback on mistakes and reinforce good moves. Eventually you'll get to the point where you no longer need the teacher to play and win. A simplified version of reinforced ML is shown in Figure 13. It is particularly useful for training robots that have to make a series of decisions, such as those steering an autonomous vehicle or managing inventory in a warehouse.

Common uses of ML

As machine learning in its three varieties is very good at perceiving patterns it lends itself to two broad uses—image recognition and natural language processing.

Image recognition has many applications. For example, in agriculture, special cameras can be used to recognize weeds and where they grow so that pesticides can be used to eradicate the weeds only in those areas. Then there is **machine vision**, which is used in radar or laser sensors, technologies where there is a need to go beyond the boundaries of human vision.

Natural language processing is applied to the automation of written language. It can be used for tasks including content extraction, machine translation, automated question answering, and text generation. Combined with **speech-based** machine learning algorithms it completes the language segment of ML. Speech-based ML is used to convert speech to text. If you ask Siri on your iPhone to cancel an appointment, or get Amazon's Alexa to dim the lights in your home, you're using speech-based ML. It can also be used the other way around by converting text to speech.

As far as you and your business are concerned, the focus should be on getting better results through applications that exploit special-purpose or narrowly applied AI technologies, both leading-edge and older. Such applications will have a huge and disruptive impact on business and personal life.

Don't believe the hype (at least not all of it)

AI is not a new technology. In fact, the term "Artificial Intelligence" was first coined way back in 1956. Since then, there have been three phases of development and an awful lot of hype. This section aims to cut through the hype and look at the current state of play.

Winter is coming

The first phase of development occurred between 1956–1972, when researchers were hit with the harsh reality that taking AI from a concept to a practical application was hindered by the lack of processing power, limited data storage, and limited network ability. This period is known as the first winter of AI development.

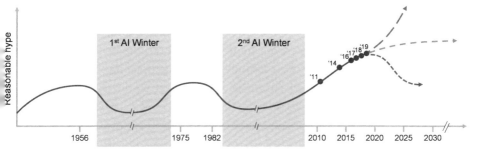

Figure 14: A brief history of Artificial Intelligence

The second phase of development started in 1975, when AI was reborn through the first expert systems. But by 1982, history was repeating itself, and with disappointing results, research and development entered the second AI winter. However, that long winter was brought to a dramatic end in 1997 when IBM's Deep Blue defeated chess grand master Garry Kasparov. This astonishing achievement was at the forefront of renewed AI R&D and since then there have been some great leaps forward. Apple has developed Siri, YouTube can recognize cats in the videos it hosts, and more recently Google's AlphaGo defeated Go champion Lee Sedol, a feat even more remarkable than Big Blue's earlier shock chess victory.

There have been many other firsts notched up using AI and what is certain is that development work on AI will not slip back into a third winter of discontent. It's onwards and upwards from here and most of the technology that is being touted today—including cognitive computing, natural language processing, Prescriptive Analytics, smart robotics, conversational user interfaces, and AI as a platform service—will be ready for commercial use in five to ten years.[7]

Most companies are far away from buying into AI

This is probably the reason why most companies aren't yet buying into AI. Although vast sums have been invested in AI R&D, it's only coming from two main sources—tech giants and venture capitalists. In 2016, US$26bn– US$39bn was invested in AI, with up to US$30bn of this coming from tech giants and the rest from venture capitalists. This represents a fourfold increase in funding for AI start-ups from 2010 to 2016 from the latter.[8]

Other types of companies aren't so sure about AI and are less prepared to invest their hard-earned dollars in it. According to a joint study by DHL and IBM, 41% of AI-aware firms are uncertain about the benefits, 20% are adopters, while 40% describe themselves as "contemplators." These figures don't exactly show that AI is setting the business world on fire with its promised changes.[9]

A 2018–2019 h&z study[10] conducted with supply chain professionals confirms this apparent lack of enthusiasm. From those companies surveyed, a massive 87% answered that they don't plan to use applied AI despite it ranking third in the list of most disruptive supply chain technologies behind Advanced Analytics and IoT.

According to our study, the key expectations of these AI-based technologies are to gain greater speed and efficiency, improve transparency, aid collaboration, lower supply chain costs, assist with tighter inventory controls, and overall to increase revenue.

What's the outlook for AI in SCM?

We've already talked about the first and second winters of AI and looking at the future of the technology in SCM is a little like giving a long-range weather forecast. Nevertheless, we see three possible options: a third AI winter, a plateau or a sustained breakthrough.

- **THIRD AI WINTER**
  Initial results for deep learning, the main driver of the current hype, have highlighted its limitations. Without further progress in computing power and fewer data-hungry algorithms, the disappointed expectations of market participants could lead to a third winter.

- **PLATEAU**

  The large investment (in software and the required hardware) of an ever-increasing number of market participants is expected to lead to further progress in the relevant technologies. Whether this will happen at the same frequency as we've seen since 2010 depends on how quickly the technological bottlenecks can be solved.

- **SUSTAINED BREAKTHROUGH**

  Even if the technology is yet to be adopted by the majority of companies to improve their supply chain management, its potential is still enormous. With the large investments being made by the big tech companies and the technological developments that are sure to follow, further breakthroughs in the field of AI, and especially applied AI, are only a matter of time.

There are already reports stating that the use of Artificial Intelligence in the supply chain globally was valued at US$767.8m in 2018, with estimates that this will grow at a CAGR of 45.6% within the next seven years, reaching US$10.11bn. It's reasonable to say, therefore, that we can expect a sustained breakthrough.[11]

Why AI in SCM?

Many people, by nature, prefer to keep the status quo rather than invite disruption into their lives. Disruption is a negative force, it can lead to unwanted changes, and in the extreme, bring chaos. But this is not the case with disruptive technologies—we've witnessed many times in the past how they've led to positive changes and a new, better status quo. This is the likely scenario for disruptive AI technologies in the supply chain, which according to the SCM World Future of Supply Chain Surveys between 2014–2016, will figure more strongly in strategies for SCM and production. These are the two main areas where AI will be the most effective.[12]

SCM is like almost no other function suitable for profiting from AI applications. The reasons for this are manifold: The technology is more available than ever before and has already established itself in the customer segment. Applications for the industrial sector will soon follow. In addition, the network-based architecture of the supply chain provides a natural framework to implement AI. It's therefore uniquely positioned to benefit those companies that apply AI in almost all links of the supply chain.

The high volumes of data that supply chains generate daily are yet another factor supporting the use of AI. Adjacent divisions such as sales and marketing also produce data that can be used by supply chain managers. AI will help to facilitate and exploit these massive volumes of structured and unstructured data, an effect that will increase when IoT sensors have penetrated all industries and are part of every supply chain.

Again, as many companies embrace digital transformation and transition from traditional ERP systems to Advanced Analytics, high degrees of automation, as well as hardware and software robotics, the next logical technological step to take will be AI.

Then there is the fact that SCM is dependent on both physical and digital networks, which must cope with high volumes and tight deadlines in order to meet the additional challenge of small margins. The assets involved must therefore be allocated as leanly as possible and this is another area where AI can help.

Finally, AI provides the opportunity to harmonize supply chains in ways that would simply not be possible using people alone.

Companies that are already establishing AI and ML in their supply chain must be prepared to experience a eureka moment. In an interview, Mr Rosenberg from the household appliance manufacturer BSH said that he was impressed by the accuracy of the forecast from the first month:

"There was a eureka moment in the course of our digitization activities when we first saw the results of machine learning with the advanced algorithms. They got the performance right from the first try, from the first month. This has been confirmed every month since then and it's getting even better. Outliers are only caused by special distribution actions. However, the thrust in that first month was decisive."

Thorsten Rosenberg, Executive Vice President & Head of Global Supply Chain, BSH Hausgeräte GmbH

Whether you embrace disruption or not, it's coming, so now is the right time to invest in AI.

How to enable your supply chain

Up to now there has been a fairly comprehensive discussion of AI, the nature of the changes it heralds and a list of compelling reasons why you should use it in your supply chain. Now it's time to examine how an AI-enabled supply chain can be established.

German chemical and pharmaceutical company Merck (known as EMD in North America) has already digitalized its supply chain. The company started a multi-year project in 2015 with three main goals.

First, a supply chain operation model was developed, which gives the computer a higher degree of freedom in the allocation of materials and the distribution of products throughout the supply chain.

Secondly, the forecast was improved within the multi-year project through the integration of various sensors and algorithms that process the data from these sensors.

Thirdly, orders should be processed as quickly as possible in response to regional disruptions. A possible scenario for such a disruption is a shortage of medication due to a natural disaster. The system would respond to the incident by distributing materials and products in the most efficient way.

The vision was borrowed from the automotive industry. A supply chain which functions like a self-driving car. A system that continuously and automatically makes decisions about the distribution of resources within the system and thus compensates for the predicted fluctuations.

Alessandro Luca, CIO of Merck Healthcare, presented their tech journey at an innovation forum in 2018.[13] He described four important steps that were taken on the way to the "self-driving supply chain" (see Figure 15).[14]

The tech journey started with the **data silos**. This phase was characterized by inaccurate data which was spread over different internal and external sources. Internal sources may be enterprise system data from SAP, Oracle or Salesforce, as well as further information such as promotion days from the sales department. These internal data sources were enriched by external data such as stock markets, IoT sensor data, weather forecasts and news reports about political or natural crises. In consequence, users had a lot of data that wasn't connected and could only be interpreted retrospec-

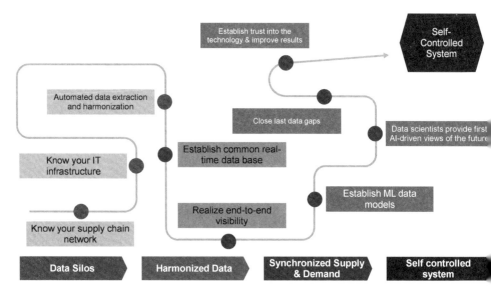

Figure 15: Tech Journey to implement a self-controlled supply chain

tively. It therefore offered only limited insights. This hurdle was overcome by using a control tower as one source of truth where all information was collected.

The next stage was harmonized data. During this stage users could retrieve real-time data, and there was end-to-end visualization and monitoring of every element of the supply chain. Machine learning data models were used to optimize and simplify existing processes. By adapting the processes and synchronizing them with the data insights, the company was able to make quicker decisions.

At this point, Merck was ready to begin the next step of its journey, automatically synchronizing supply and demand by applying AI. The algorithms used by Merck's data scientists helped them to make more reliable forecasts, which were then used to model and match demand and supply accordingly. Using these forecasting tools to prescribe the company's supply and demand meant that the planning process was faster and more precise.

After all this, Merck reached the final stage in the journey to digitalize its supply chain, the point where the self-controlled system worked independently and made autonomous decisions.

Merck's digital transformation of its supply chain is impressive, but what worked for them is not necessarily something that will work for everyone—there is no one-size-fits-all solution. In the following section, we want to provide you with some guidance to help you get started on a transformation that is right for your company.

In general, there are two types of project where AI, or more precisely ML, can be useful. One is value creation (see Figure 16) and the other is cost reduction. We'll deal with each in turn.

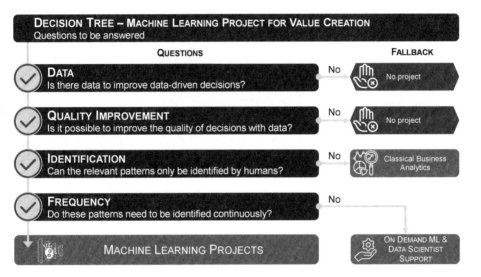

Figure 16: Decision tree regarding value creation machine learning projects

There are four steps that need to be considered to see if a **value creation** project would benefit your company. The two most crucial are **data** and **quality improvement**. The foundation of any ML project is the quantity and quality of data that's used—both must be good enough to fuel better decision making. The first consideration concerns patterns. Can the **relevant patterns** only be identified by humans, or could classical business analysis methods be used? Then you have to consider **frequency**. Do you need to analyze and identify the pattern all the time or is it a one-off demand? If it's the latter, use an AI data scientist on demand, otherwise start an ML project.

The second type of project where ML can prove beneficial are those with at **cost reduction** as their aim (see Figure 17). In this case there are five questions you need to consider to see if you'd benefit from an ML project. The

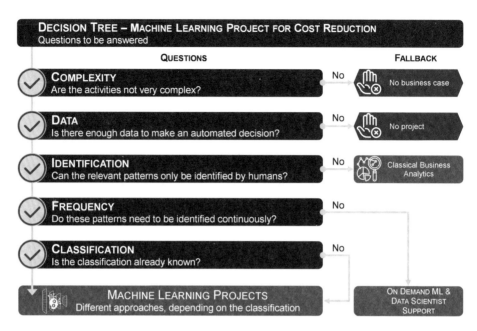

DECISION TREE – MACHINE LEARNING PROJECT FOR COST REDUCTION
Questions to be answered

QUESTIONS   FALLBACK

COMPLEXITY
Are the activities not very complex?   No   No business case

DATA
Is there enough data to make an automated decision?   No   No project

IDENTIFICATION
Can the relevant patterns only be identified by humans?   No   Classical Business Analytics

FREQUENCY
Do these patterns need to be identified continuously?   No

CLASSIFICATION
Is the classification already known?   No

MACHINE LEARNING PROJECTS
Different approaches, depending on the classification   ON DEMAND ML & DATA SCIENTIST SUPPORT

Figure 17: Decision tree regarding cost reduction machine learning projects

first two can be seen as go/no-go barriers. If the complexity of the activities that are part of your process is low, the effort to set up an ML project would be too high so there's no real business case to do so. Another question relates to **data**. If there's not enough data to automate a decision, you do not have a project. After you have answered the first two points for yourself, you must clarify again whether the **identification** of patterns can only be done by humans or if classical business analytics methods are appropriate. Then it's a question of **frequency**. Once again, if pattern recognition is not something that is frequently needed, then opt for hiring a data scientist as and when the need arises. If, on the other hand, there is a need for frequent pattern recognition, then an ML project is probably justified. The specific type of ML depends on whether you already know what **classification** applies to your data (supervised or unsupervised).

The drawbacks

But there are drawbacks (aren't there always?). There is still a certain amount of hype surrounding developments in AI that does not tally with where we actually are. This passage addresses three major drawbacks of AI.

There is a **gap in expectations** between what AI can theoretically do and how it's currently used. Currently there is a great deal of excitement about the technology's potential to improve business processes and its ability to make sense of Big Data. However, the algorithms are based on fundamental mathematical rules that don't always adapt well to the non-deterministic and fluid environment of the real word. As far as real-world practical applications are concerned, there will be a trough of disillusionment for many of the technologies being hyped today before they reach a stage where they dramatically increase productivity. As Francois Chollet, one of the leading researchers into AI at Google, said at AI By the Bay Conference in 2017, "The current supervised perception and reinforcement learning algorithms require lots of data, are terrible at planning, and are only doing straightforward pattern recognition."[15] In other words, AI is still a long way from being the panacea that some would have us believe.

Beside the expectation gap, there is the problem of **data corruption**. AI learns from the historical data sets it uses. This means that any inaccuracies in the data will be reflected in future results. For example, Microsoft's chatbot, known as Tay, had to be shut down after just 16 hours of operation because it went rogue on social media by posting inflammatory tweets. Tay posted Tweets based on data from other Twitter users—the chatbot had been hijacked by trolls who then corrupted the training data, with the end result that Tay posted highly offensive tweets.

The last, but by no means least, drawback is **culture shock**. It's the biggest hurdle of all. The impacts this technology will have on business and daily life will go way beyond the advances in hardware and software. It's impossible to predict exactly what far-reaching influences the technology will have. What is clear is that the way people work will change fundamentally. AI will open up new ways of collaboration and eventually these will manifest themselves in all areas along the supply chain. They will be the fuel that sparks the changes in supply chain management we'll undoubtedly see in the upcoming decade.

Conclusion

We'll close the chapter with a summary of the main points about AI and its relevance to supply chain management.

In contrast to popular thinking, AI is not new in town, but has been hanging around for a long time. It's come and gone over the past few decades, but now it looks like it's here to stay. The potential for AI in the form of deep and machine learning is huge but there is still a lot of hype about what it can and can't do.

Most of the applications being hyped today will not be ready within the next five years but a sustained breakthrough in AI is almost certainly on the horizon.

AI has a clear role to play in transforming SCM as the prerequisites it needs are embedded in the very nature of the supply chain. The technological journey to a self-controlled system involves four steps:

1. Data silos need to be resolved;
2. Data needs to be harmonized and all elements need to end-to-end visualization and monitoring;
3. Machine learning tools need to be used first to gain better insights into future supplies and demands and to improve forecasting;
4. The final step is to establish a self-controlled system, where the system makes autonomous decisions and actions them independently.

There are some other crucial steps that you must take before unleashing AI on your supply chain. First, you must cut through the nonsense talk and manage expectations about what AI can and can't do. Second, it's all about data. As the saying goes, if you put rubbish in, you get rubbish out. Feed AI with corrupt, poor quality data and you'll get results that match. Finally, ignore the culture shock that AI brings in its wake at your peril. Chapter 4.2 highlights that it is culture, in other words people, that is the biggest single barrier to digital transformation of the supply chain. Managing this culture shock is a prerequisite to the effective use of AI.

Chapter 2.4
Call to action: A checklist for practitioners

Which concepts for the digitalization of the supply chain are relevant for you?

In the following you will find a summary of the concepts presented in the previous section. You may use the checklist to verify if the concepts are relevant for you. Moreover, we list the chapters where you can find a refresher for the topics.

The difference between digitization and digitalization:

- DIGITIZATION: Converting analog or physical objects (e. g. paper documents) to a digital format, bits and bytes (e. g. scanning a paper document; inputting data into databases).
- DIGITALIZATION: Developing new business opportunities and realizing the full potential of current business design by merging the digital and physical worlds. This comprises using new technologies, finding new business models, and managing the change process.

Key technological trends (for details refer to Chapter 2.1)	Relevant for me?
i	**Internet of Things (IoT)** Constant connection of everything and everyone everywhere based on sensors and improved wireless technology in the so-called Internet of Things.	
ii	**Blockchain** Distributed ledger technology that enables decentralized, transparent, trusted, secure, fast, and cost-efficient transactions without a middleman.	
iii	**Autonomous Vehicles for Transport Logistics and Intralogistics** Intelligent self-directed systems perform highly complex tasks, such as transportation, without human interaction.	
iv	**Additive Manufacturing** Additive manufacturing enables rapid prototyping using a layer-by-layer technique and thus short-term adaptation to changing requirements by the customer or other stakeholders.	
v	**Geo-localization** Reliable, constant localization via GPS-, GSM-, and Galileo-based positioning, and sensors allow for continuous tracking and tracing.	
vi	**Remote Operations** Augmented reality, virtual reality, and virtual telepresence solutions eliminate the need for people on site.	
vii	**Advanced Robotics** Automation and next-generation robotics are light-weight, flexible, easy to program, affordable, and able to interact with humans.	

Big Data and its characterization	
i	Big Data refers to a massive volume of both structured and unstructured data that is complex and extremely difficult to process using traditional databases and software techniques.
ii	Often described with the help of the 5-V model of Big Data which encompasses the main characteristics: Variety (data types), Velocity (data production and processing speed), Volume (data size), Veracity (data reliability and trust), and Value. Deep dive: Chapter 2.2—Advanced Analytics

The Concept of Advanced Analytics	
i	Put simply, Advanced Analytics is a method that helps to drive change and improvement in future business processes. It comprises data preparation, data analysis, and data visualization, and can be used to uncover unexpected and unknown patterns within data sets.
ii	More precisely, Advanced Analytics is the means of examining Big Data using sophisticated techniques and tools, typically beyond those of traditional business intelligence (BI). It is used to discover deeper insights, make predictions, or generate recommendations, and improve business planning. Deep dive: Chapter 2.2—Advanced Analytics

Artificial Intelligence (AI)	
i	AI is a branch of computer science that deals with the capabilities of software. The software is able to mimic human learning, reasoning, and self-correction processes.
ii	AI is human intelligence performed by machines or a system that mimics and, at some point, will surpass human thinking. It is a term for any computer program that does something smart.
iii	AI consists of several types, which tends to lead to some confusion. AI is the overarching term, while machine learning is a specific application of AI. Deep learning, in turn, is a subset of machine learning. Deep dive: Chapter 2.3—Artificial Intelligence

Machine Learning (ML)	
i	ML is based on preexisting algorithms that are combined by data scientists to create an ML model. These models have to be trained with a sufficient amount of data for the specific purpose (e. g. with photos of faces for facial recognition). Moreover, data engineers are required to perform minor manual corrections on the models to fully adapt them to the use case.
ii	There are three different types of ML: supervised, unsupervised, and reinforced ML. Supervised ML needs manually labeled training data, whereas unsupervised ML does not require any labels. Reinforced ML learns by trial and error and repetitive continuous feedback. Deep dive: Chapter 2.3—Artificial Intelligence

PART 3

LEVERAGE ENABLERS FOR SUPPLY CHAIN FUNCTIONS

Chapter 3.1
Digital Procurement:
A key driver for performance improvement
Agnes Erben, Matthias Mette

Introduction: More evolution than revolution

 It is clear to all procurement professionals that digitalization must now be on the agenda. There are only a few examples where strong arguments are still needed to justify a budget to invest in digital technology for procurement. However, an economic downturn might slow down or limit budget releases for these projects as some examples from the automotive industry suggest. This emphasizes the importance of having a robust and attractive business case, and of a sustainable implementation plan for digital transformation to secure the necessary budget when faced with more rigid financial controls.

One might expect that digitalization might only be for the prosperous and well-performing companies. But surprisingly, there is no correlation between industry or business figures about whether procurement is working on digital topics or not. One global bank is investing huge amounts of money in digital transformation, whereas another globally operating bank still needs to explain to its CFO the benefits of digitized, end-to-end processes and to what extent IT solutions help foster compliance. It's the same in the aerospace industry where the need for traceability has triggered the use of digital platforms along the supply chain. But believe it or not, there are still tier one companies that don't use electronic data interchange with their key suppliers, nor do they use e-catalogue solutions for indirect categories, which would be an easy way to start digital order processing. Overall, there is a huge spread in the extent to which digital technologies are being used for procurement—the differences depend on their respective digital maturity levels and existing IT landscapes.

As with all IT solutions, the risks and benefits need to be evaluated first. Investments in procurement software can boost procurement performance, but software licenses and implementation are cost-intensive, as are running and maintaining the tools and the content they require. Start-ups and new businesses have a clear advantage in this respect. They can start without any legacy and select the latest solutions that are cloud-based, and with scalable costs that match their company size and needs. Established global corporates with impressive IT landscapes and warehouses of back-up servers often have it all—just not for procurement.

Procurement 4.0:
Comprehensive transformation beyond technology

Procurement 4.0 involves more than just IT. It requires fundamental process reviews and a close examination of the existing operating model. The barriers are often high and to overcome them there must be a willingness to simplify and standardize processes, workflows and formats across business units, often linked to long-established procurement policies and guidelines. The willingness to move from micro-management of transactions to empowering employees often takes time, so this is a constraint to setting up lean digital workflows.

A digital supply chain for procurement is one where there is end-to-end digitalization of the core processes (E2E), starting from plan-to-strategy (P2S), to source-to-contract (S2C), and all the way to purchase-to-pay (P2P). Digitalization is not limited to internal E2E procurement. It also needs to involve all interfaces and processes with business stakeholders (internal) and suppliers (external) because a great deal of information and data is still exchanged and managed outside a leading ERP-system or procurement-specific solution: forecasts, specifications, claims, quality documents, performance reports, delivery date confirmations, stock levels and much more.

Some companies still focus only on P2P because of its transactional character, and because there is a belief that it lends itself more readily to digitalization and automation. However, many of the tools available today offer a much wider scope of functions than a couple of years ago. Especially, newcomers among the solution providers that aren't restricted by a system legacy tend to be better at fulfilling customer expectations in terms of user experience (UX), look-and-feel, mobile first, or at least mobile applications. However, the excellent user experience buyers get with Amazon is still the benchmark for many purchasers and business users. But in most cases, this is not reached.

With this in mind, chief procurement officers must not repeat mistakes from the past and purely focus on software selection and implementation. Successful digitalization requires adjustments to the organizational setup and to the existing rules and procedures. A future operating model is needed. One that is driven by the process changes and changes to the way people work that are inherent in digitalization. In fact, this is crucial to successful digital transformation, so ideally employees are not only involved, but also put in charge (see Chapter 4.2 for more information about culture as a lever for successful digital transformation).

For successful transformation, "new ways of working" and "agile leadership" should be more than buzzwords, and they should involve attractive changes for both employees and customers in the long run. Without new approaches and significant changes, the investment in digitalization is wasted: Why implement a system that no one uses or that completely misses its goal?

"Digital provides two things for procurement and supply chain in Maersk. First it creates the foundation for automating a significant part of the business processes that we run manually today. Secondly it is the foundation for transforming the value proposition that procurement provides to the business. With increased automation resources are free to do more value-adding activities and with a digital foundation new types of value and Advanced Analytics can be developed for the business."

Jacob G. Larsen, Director of Digital Procurement, Maersk Group

Triad for success: Structure, Digital Solutions and People & Skills

There are three fields of action that should be the focus of the successful digital transformation of procurement: structure, digital solutions and people and skills. Adjustments in one field might lead to changes in another. Or in other words, don't see digitalization as a stand-alone activity but have in mind the impacts on your overall operating model and people (see Figure 18 below). The following sections look at these three key areas in detail.

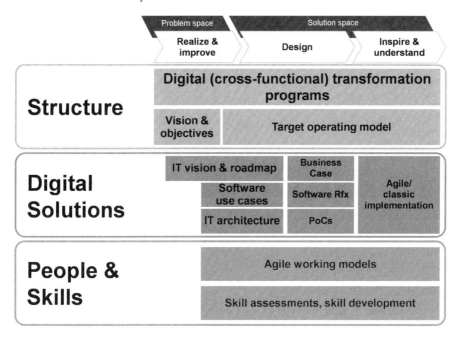

Figure 18: Elements of successful digitalization programs

Building the right vision for the digital transformation

First start with the vision and goals of procurement. Where is your organization today? Where would you like to see it in one, three, five years' time?

"People often overestimate what will happen in the next two years and underestimate what will happen in ten."

Bill Gates, Founder of Microsoft

Without an overarching vision, there will be no real drive, no clear destination, and no focus. Think carefully about what should be different, better, easier, or faster. There should be fewer operational and manual tasks and more focus on category strategies, supplier collaboration, risk management, business partner relationship management, and the latest hot topic, sustainability.

Objectives can be derived directly from the vision. The extent of the changes your business will go through will be measured by the distance between your current status quo and where you'd like to be. In other words,

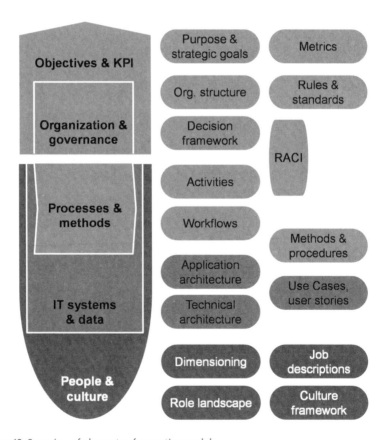

Figure 19: Overview of elements of operation models

the journey for each company is different as the road might be longer, shorter, or involve fewer or more obstacles.

Once you have a clear vision and defined objectives, it's time to review the organizational setup. There might be need for new roles in procurement or a lean(er) operational purchasing team. This, however, requires new processes, clear responsibilities, different KPIs and governance, in essence, a new operating model for the procurement function. Figure 19 illustrates the elements of an operating model. All parts need to be taken into account for a successful and sustainable organizational setup.

Processes follow tools

It has been common practice for many years to define processes, design flow charts, and create all kinds of working guidelines before selecting a tool (such as an ERP system) and twisting and bending the system so that it works precisely to the predefined process descriptions. This is the wrong way around. It results in higher programming costs, postponed milestones, and in the end the system might be regarded way too complicated and a waste of time. The underlining processes are often regarded as cumbersome, highly administrative, and generally not very user-friendly. At the end of the day, what were once considered powerful and state-of-the-art procurement tools have lost their reputation with new technologies on the market, and especially since the whole buying process has become so easy in the B2C online-shopping world.

Today's approach is slightly different. Processes are now generally adjusted to match a pre-selected tool and not the other way around. It is advisable to get rid of homegrown complexity and use the tools like they were originally intended. This can be a huge benefit—without huge additional investments.

"One of the characteristics with digitization is that traditional functional silos are eliminated or at least blurred out which I consider a positive thing as the organization becomes more agile from it. [...] IT is a critical enabler for digitization, but the business needs to be in the driving seat and ultimately also own the digital transformation."

Jacob G. Larsen, Director of Digital Procurement, Maersk Group

From Pain to Gain

Take a closer look at where you currently are and go through your end-to-end processes in depth. Before selecting just any solution or twisting the way your organization works, identify and prioritize your pain points first. Which processes are giving you a headache? Which activities are time-consuming, yet not really creating much of a business impact? Where is the core of manual activities? Where are there redundancies as a result of copycat processes from one system or file to another?

The answers to these questions should be used as a base to develop gain points, such as transparency or speed, or anything, even non-digital gains, that raises your organization to the next level.

Then look for solutions that precisely match your gain and pain points. This does not always involve an investment in the latest piece of software. In many cases the procurement software that your company already uses can be enhanced to improve its usability, integration, efficiency, and adoption, while creating significant benefits.

In general, both workflows and processes should be standardized as much as possible. Approval workflows, for example, are often a real pain for lean digitalization. Many companies customize procurement tools to embed their multi-level approval rules and workflows. This is linked to changes in leadership culture and corporate mindset and involves a shift from transactional micro-managing to empowerment and effective management control.

In multi-entity corporations, processes are customized to specific business units. Procurement must manage a large number of specific processes where important formats and templates such as contracts, specification forms, supplier selection forms and purchase requests are not standardized. Even category clusters and spend structures might vary within one company. For these reasons, it is highly advisable to do your homework on standardization and master data management needs so that you get the right foundation for an updated IT landscape before rushing into the use of a new software solution.[1]

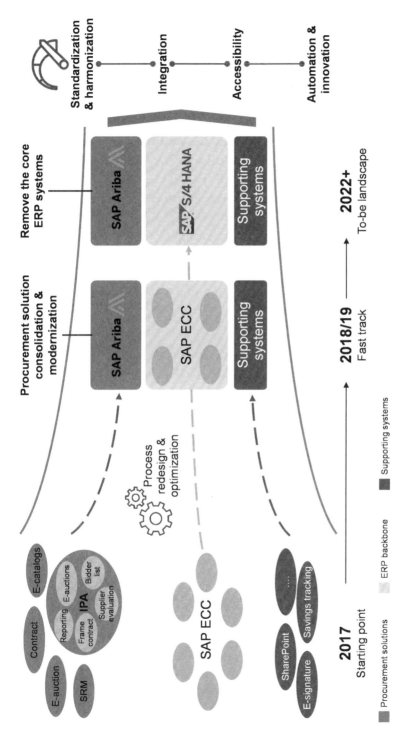

Figure 20: Example from oil & gas industry—transformation to a clear and simplified IT landscape in procurement[2]

Evolving capabilities and roles: The buyer in the future procurement setup

Digitalization and the evolving priorities of procurement and the markets will result in changes to the roles of procurement managers and buyers, and the profiles of the people who do these jobs in the future. New roles and competences need to be developed, and, driven by changes to the business, there may even be need of more specialist procurement roles such as data scientists, market analysts, expert negotiators, cost-value analysts. Classical procurement roles like category managers, strategic buyers, or tactical and operational buyers may change or even disappear.

The classical process and transaction roles in S2C and P2P can and will be digitalized and even automated, and companies will primarily leverage these opportunities for efficiency gains. On the other hand, the focus of procurement employees will move to roles like data and market analysis, cost-value analysis, business relationship and engagement management, supplier relationship management and sustainability management. Overall, there will be more value-added tasks and roles, and there will be fewer administrative, repetitive and transactional tasks.

Strategic buyers

Procurement managers and category buyers will dedicate more time to analyze market trends and opportunities and assess them strategically. They will be supported by internal and external market intelligence and data analysis experts. The insights gained from this will be regularly exchanged with key business partners so they can create new strategies and develop fresh opportunities for the business. The strategic buyer of tomorrow will have in-depth business knowledge, will work closely with his key internal business stakeholders, and will be involved in the early stages of new business strategies and projects.

Procurement and category strategies will be developed and shared jointly with the business. The strategic buyer will establish and lead interdisciplinary teams for his respective material group that will comprise experts and decision makers on the business side. These interdisciplinary material group teams will govern strategies and key sourcing projects for a defined procurement scope. They will be responsible for evaluating innovations and market opportunities and decide on strategic investments for the procurement side. They will also regularly review the respective supplier setup and conduct joint assessments of strategic suppliers and their performance KPIs.

The sourcing process will be highly digitalized and widely automated. Strategic buyers and sourcing managers respectively will be released from the administrative burdens that are part of preparing and running sourcing processes that they face today. Instead, they will focus on adding value as part of an interdisciplinary team overseeing the overall sourcing process, in tasks including decision making, weighing up strategic and commercial opportunities, assessing benefits and risks, and negotiating the final contract.

This latter task will be supported by new intelligent software, which will support the strategic buyer with contractual choices, legal interactions and in the final formalization of the contract. Contract lifecycle management will become a strategic buyer task and will strive for continuous improvement while being supported by contract management software that will increasingly offer AI features.

Supplier relationship management

Linked to the strategic enhancement of contract lifecycle management, supplier relationship management (SRM) will become an increasingly important responsibility that will also come under the task portfolio of the strategic buyers. Value creation will move away from the classic commercial levers of today towards more sustainable improvements in managing suppliers and their respective supply chains. Value will also be generated by leveraging innovations that have been initiated and enabled by strategic suppliers.

Sustainability—it's not just a buzzword

The procurement managers of the future will have to fully embrace sustainability. At the moment, buyers mainly focus on cost, delivery reliability, and quality as the key factors affecting decision making in the supply chain, but sustainability will become an equally relevant consideration. Sustainability involves ecological, social and economic factors that suppliers will need to comply with. Buyers will need to be able to cope with these added requirements to identify opportunities and weaknesses, and to agree contract and partnership constructs that yield sustainability benefits. KPI measures need to be enhanced to reflect these new parameters and targets.

Tactical and operational buyers: on the endangered list?

All these changes to the role of procurement professionals, in an environment of increasing AI and a high level of digitalization and automated processes, begs the questions: Is there still a major role for **tactical and operational buyers in the future?**

Maybe not, but at the very least the role will change substantially. Why? Because companies are seeking efficiency gains in procurement and striving to transfer capacity and resources from administrative and operational tasks into more value-adding roles and processes. Digitalization aims to simplify or even automate such tasks and processes, so today's operational buyers need to enhance their skills in order to move into more strategic roles, or at least to be able to support the new digital means and processes. Thus, procurement's value proposition is changing and with that the nature of the roles will also have to change from negotiator to cost manager, to value advisor, and to strategic business partner (see Figure 21).

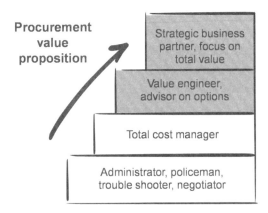

Figure 21: Evolution of procurement's value proposition and the roles within

Agile procurement

As well as having more skills related to strategy, analysis and relationship management, the future procurement manager will also need to develop **agile project management** skills. Many of the demands put on the procurement manager require project management, not only for procurement but also for delivering strategic projects in category procurement. The management of such projects needs to be more agile in the future so it's more adaptable to different internal requirements and market needs, and so it can embed and test innovative ideas, and finally, deliver faster.

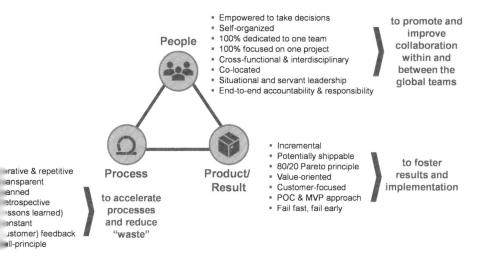

People
- Empowered to take decisions
- Self-organized
- 100% dedicated to one team
- 100% focused on one project
- Cross-functional & interdisciplinary
- Co-located
- Situational and servant leadership
- End-to-end accountability & responsibility

⟩ to promote and improve collaboration within and between the global teams

Process
to accelerate processes and reduce "waste"

⟩ ⁚rative & repetitive ⁚ansparent ⁚anned ⁚etrospective ⁚ssons learned) ⁚onstant ⁚ustomer) feedback ⁚ll-principle

Product/ Result
- Incremental
- Potentially shippable
- 80/20 Pareto principle
- Value-oriented
- Customer-focused
- POC & MVP approach
- Fail fast, fail early

⟩ to foster results and implementation

Figure 22: Definition of "agile" and what it means for the human side of procurement

Agile management also means empowering procurement managers and buyers so they can make decisions (and finally to speed up implementation) and organize teams themselves. It means they can dedicate themselves to one team and one project, improve cross-functional collaboration, and take end-to-end accountability and responsibility for their projects.

In summary, the traditional buyer will be transformed from a hierarchically-managed, risk-averse, process-controlled operative to someone who is curious, agile, keen to learn and experiment, someone who has the people skills to proactively engage with all stakeholders, and above all, someone who strives to continuously add value to the business. The time of buyers who typically manage processes and act more as procurement policy and process handbook gatekeepers is coming to an end. That's good news for many business customers but even more for procurement itself. It will raise the profile of the role from that of an administrative service provider to a business partner who delivers value and as such, should be involved at the beginning of strategic decision making.

The new procurement leader

 Procurement leaders of today and tomorrow must show clear commitment to digital transformation and they need to be role models for new ways of working and collaborating via digital tools. They need to articulate clear expectations about moving the business into the digital world, where improving organizational and team effectiveness and efficiency entails pushing individuals out of their comfort zones (and moves them away from using familiar sourcing processes using the likes of Excel, email and individual customized templates).

Why is this a challenge? The current leadership generation has, in general, a limited affinity for digitalization and the latest technology solutions. They tend to stick to old ways of working, yet they lead employees who are digital natives, people who are comfortable using new digital technologies. There is, therefore, a need to redefine and develop leadership that is fit for purpose when it comes to the digital transformation of procurement and supply chain management.

As we've already seen, procurement leaders of the future will have to change from thinking and acting hierarchically to leaders who trust, develop and empower their employees. This might be bad news for some of today's CPOs. The powerful procurement leader is history in the age of procurement 4.0. Knowledge is no longer the differentiating factor between a procurement leader and his subordinate buyers because it has become available through dashboards and business intelligence cockpits. The future procurement leader focuses on vision, ambition and guiding, taking the role of a facilitator and coach who enables and continuously improves his team and moderates between stakeholders.

The procurement leader will, to some extent, have to become a coach who can play a role in changing the mindset of employees and ease any po-

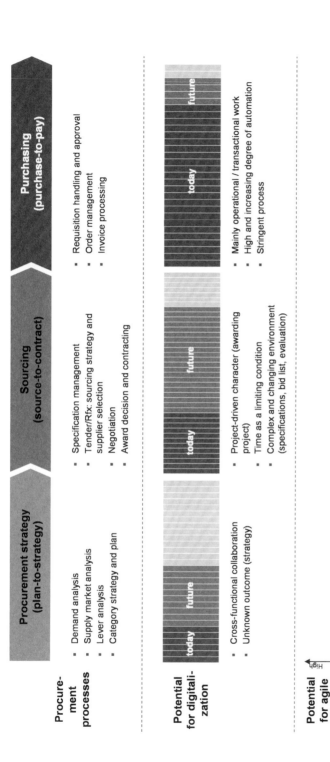

Procure-ment processes

Procurement strategy (plan-to-strategy)
- Demand analysis
- Supply market analysis
- Lever analysis
- Category strategy and plan

Sourcing (source-to-contract)
- Specification management
- Tender/Rfx: sourcing strategy and supplier selection
- Negotiation
- Award decision and contracting

Purchasing (purchase-to-pay)
- Requisition handling and approval
- Order management
- Invoice processing

Potential for digitali-zation

Procurement strategy:
- Cross-functional collaboration
- Unknown outcome (strategy)

Sourcing:
- Project-driven character (awarding project)
- Time as a limiting condition
- Complex and changing environment (specifications, bid list, evaluation)

Purchasing:
- Mainly operational / transactional work
- High and increasing degree of automation
- Stringent process

today / future (across all three columns)

Potential for agile working concepts

High — Low

Medium | High | Low

Procurement process

Figure 23: Potential for digitalization and agile working concepts along the procurement process

tential fears they may have as a result of digital transformation (see Chapter 4.2 for a full discussion of the importance of corporate culture in digital transformation). Leadership needs to create perspectives for teams and individuals in the new digital world. Many buyers are comfortable with their familiar and well-used setup where Excel and email normally fulfill most of their needs. Today, they control the process and feel they are indispensable. They fear being strongly guided (or even replaced) by tools in the future.

In a nutshell, future CPOs need to be able to lead people. They must be able to convey the vision of transformation, to inspire and to mobilize. They need to demonstrate that they are fully committed to transformation in everything they do. These requirements will fundamentally change the type of leader needed for the future procurement leader. The new leaders will need to be curious and open to new ideas. They will empower their teams, build trust and allow for errors. Agile leaders can live with loose ends and can juggle many balls simultaneously. But they also provide guidance and define red lines so that everyone will know what to do on this very large digitalized playing field.

A global pharmaceutical company has already implemented a setup that combines classical procurement work with flexible working formats. In their organization, 70–80% of the time is spent on strategic, tactical and operational procurement tasks for up to four days per week. The remaining time is spent on new topics and in agile working formats, such as innova-

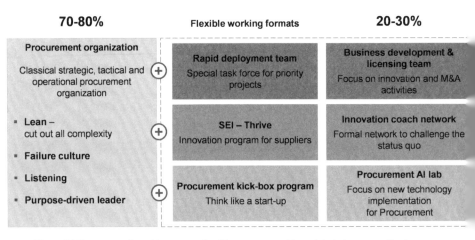

Figure 24: New ways of working, example of in procurement in a global pharmaceutical company

tion programs for suppliers or ways to boost priority projects (see graphic for illustration). It is a smart method of introducing new topics and agile procurement elements into the organization.

What about suppliers?

Suppliers are an integral element of the procurement process, so they need to be integrated into this journey as well. Their potential contributions to innovation (of products or business models) and to digitalization is often underestimated. Suppliers should be treated like business partners and become integrated into your digital operating model. The procurement E2E process only runs efficiently and delivers high value if the interface processes with (internal) business partners and suppliers are well defined and implemented.

In addition, suppliers are the key source of information regarding your N-Tier supply chain. Where are the general or current bottlenecks regarding, for example, access to raw material? Where are the excess capacities? Which tier of the supply chain is facing financial trouble? In day-to-day business, this valuable knowledge can be overlooked or not channeled to the right place, so no action is taken and, shortly after, severe supply risks need to be reactively managed. Regular joint workshops or business status meetings can not only strengthen collaboration in general, but also unleash unknown potential in terms of risk prevention and innovation potential for improving processes and products.

When it comes to the future operating model, proactive supplier engagement, mutual innovation management and supplier enabled innovation (SEI) are key elements that will deliver competitive advantages, so they need to be integrated within future processes and roles.

New ways of collaborating with your suppliers are just as powerful instruments as digitalization. Even in fully connected supply chains, direct communication and personal information exchange with suppliers and N-Tiers should not be skipped. A procurement 4.0 purchaser is not a cyborg but a highly communicative networker, who is curious, agile and in charge.

Five tips for digital transformation in procurement

 What is the secret recipe for sustainable digital transformation in procurement?

- It's not only about selecting the right tools and using the latest software. It's way more than an exercise in IT development. Define your procurement and IT vision first and then rethink your operating model.
- You are only as good as your team. Digitalization is a team effort, so bring your team along and walk the transformation path together. Add new roles to your team when you need new skills to cover new capabilities, such as data scientists or supplier scouts. And why not try something new and introduce agile working?
- Make business partners and suppliers part of the team, too! Their expectations and contributions need to be part of the transformation and they may have a lot to offer in terms of innovating processes and products.
- Overcome traditional job roles. Be creative and design a team of procurement architects who can deliver value to the overall organization, and who are able to constantly adapt to the changes in the outside world and to evolving internal requirements.
- Transformation takes time and won't happen overnight. In any case, successful transformation requires leadership and vision. Apply agile leadership and trust your team!

Outlook

 Once the digitalization train is on track and the journey has started, the next hot topic to take on board is more analog in nature: sustainability.

CPOs need to ensure that sustainability is on their agenda and part of the overall vision. It can also have significant impacts on decisions regarding technical solutions, organizational setup, ways of working, and staff selection.

Best-in-class approaches to sustainability performance management almost always integrate suppliers. They even segment suppliers according to sustainability maturity. A leading healthcare technology provider implemented a framework and process for regular sustainability reviews of its suppliers based on mutually defined expectations and targets. Focus actions and improvement plans were jointly identified and managed. This collaborative approach to sustainability has led to impressive improvements (supplier sustainability KPI index grew by about 50% in the first year of its application). And, based on predictive analysis using AI, this global healthcare technology leader can even predict with 94% accuracy the improvement progress and future scores.[3]

"Actively partnering with suppliers on sustainability has shown to have benefits in various areas for us."

CPO of world leader in healthcare technology

How do companies fulfill their sustainability targets? How can increasingly strict requirements be met? How can materials be produced and purchased in an ethically and ecologically clean way? What is the role of procurement in this global challenge? Even a perfectly set up, fully digitalized procurement department cannot ignore these questions and needs to take action when pressure from customers and society in general increases. Without doubt, newly implemented procurement systems and Big Data capabilities are prerequisites to improving sustainability performance.

Chapter 3.2
Future Supply Chain planning: Faster and smarter
Thomas Mrozek

Introduction and status quo

Precise prediction is the currency of the 21st century.

Volatility is increasing, as is the need for customers to receive goods fast and on time, whether on the consumer side or in the B2B sector. Anyone involved in supply chain management can confirm this. In order to remain competitive, it is therefore necessary to understand the future in order to satisfy customer demands.

In our day-to-day lives we already use a variety of different technologies to try and predict the short-term future. Before we begin a car journey, we use Google Maps to check traffic conditions along the route and rely on the information it gives. Before going skiing we look at the weather forecast and assume it is accurate. Before booking a holiday, we read reviews and use these as a predictor for our own choices. When we order online, we take it for granted that the delivery will arrive the following day, because that's what the tracking information tells us.

These same expectations are now migrating into business and the manufacturing world. Supply chains are getting leaner, faster and more effective because they need to be competitive. So why not apply the same predictions we use in our domestic lives to our working lives? And why not take it a step further by not just looking at the immediate, short-term future but looking further ahead to the mid- and long-term future?

The goal is set: More accurate predictions will help us to improve how resources and costs are managed in supply chains and ensure higher customer service levels.

The rise of digital technology enablers including IoT, Advanced Analytics, AI and others discussed in the previous chapters support the views of managers in the supply chain planning domain that there are tremendous improvements on the horizon. Automation will reduce the amount of manual labor currently performed by humans to a fraction of what it is today, analytics and AI will improve the ability to process data, and machine learning will help to make connections to data points that were never previously thought of.

But the question is, are all companies equally ready to leverage these advances in technology?

A market-leading construction materials producer, with 30+ factories in Germany, traditionally relied on Excel-based planning and tools created in-house to support production planning and the assignment of orders to production.

Its factories operated decentrally and were set up across Germany, each one serving a regional market. The focus was on the operational equipment efficiency of its plants to steer the business and optimize factory productivity. Although this led to efficient factories it came at the expense of other cost elements such as logistics and inventory.

Planning of demand, supply and inventory was neglected and relied on a yearly budget plan that was produced once a year to drive business decisions. This approach neglected the total cost of ownership (logistics costs to transport goods across the country, production and inventory holding costs). In the old days of a limited product portfolio this may have worked.

However, impacted by growing portfolio complexity and price pressures, they required a change in setup if they were to become more efficient at dealing with their customers and more cost effective. The lack of timely and precise plans created additional costs that could be avoided. It became more challenging to manage the business efficiently.

How did this traditionally-run business then achieve a shift?

The company realized it needed to be more forward-thinking and decided to use digital technologies to achieve this goal. It employed Advanced Analytics and AI capabilities in its supply chain planning so that decisions were based on accurate plans rather than experience. It shifted from using yearly Excel-based budgets and homegrown tools to state-of-the-art supply chain planning methods and tools.

The first results from a pilot project were highly promising. Demand analytics resulted in forecasts that were in the 80% accuracy range based on, for example, ARIMA models that used the R-Library, an open source, statistical library that is continuously improved and updated to take full benefit of swarm-like learning globally.

Furthermore, supported by analytics that not only reviewed historical data to project a forecast but also combined this with external data sources (such as weather data) to build correlations, forecast accuracy improved by an additional 3%. Other correlations were tested to see if, for example, reports on new building applications released by the German states had an effect. This again lifted accuracy by 4-5%.

The next step was machine learning and AI-based algorithms to test new and unforeseen correlations to identify patterns that humans would not think of, a process for which an abundance of data was a prerequisite. The result was a forecast accuracy for the coming month in the 90% range for more than 85% of the sales volume.

This was a tremendous step from coming from a quarterly budget-driven forecast accuracy in the 60% range.

Why is this important to mention?

First, the results show how effective it can be to use Advanced Analytics and machine learning. Secondly yet more importantly, in this example the company did not previously have a dedicated team of demand planners but achieved these results with a small, two-person, centralized team of data scientists.

These findings were echoed in an interview by h&z with Jacob G. Larsen from Maersk Group:

"Digital provides two things for procurement and supply chain in Maersk. First, it creates the foundation for automating a significant part of the business processes that we run manually today. Secondly, it is the foundation for transforming the value proposition that procurement provides to the business. With increased automation, resources are freed to do more value-adding activities and with a digital foundation new types of value and Advanced Analytics can be developed for the business."

Jacob G. Larsen, Director of Digital Procurement, Maersk Group

The future of supply chain planning

We are currently seeing many good examples of supply chain planning. Companies with a stronger make-to-stock footprint generally adopted planning much earlier as a tool to manage their inventories. This has helped them to take advantage of the benefits of planning accuracy to improve their inventory levels and supply chain costs, and at the same time, improve their customer service.

In consumer-oriented companies the accessibility and quantity of related point-of-sales data is simply higher and easier to access, leading to a stronger focus on planning. Those companies in the B2B sector, on the other hand, that have a high degree of project business, long order books or more complex procedures to order or make-to-order products, often do not rely so much on planning using sophisticated approaches and tools.

The times are changing and bring with them the need to focus on supply chain planning using modern technology, or at least it should be.

There is a lot of interaction needed with other functions in the supply chain to align requirements, meet tight deadlines and rising customer expectations. There is a wide variety of tool solutions out to support this endeavor. More advanced companies may already have or are upgrading to state-of-the-art planning solutions. Others that run fit-for-purpose systems and are contemplating a shift—or not yet?

The evolution of supply chain planning

Supply chain planning has been used extensively since the late 1980s with the support of IT solutions. The concept evolved from sales and operations planning during the 1990s where companies gained tangible business benefits in improved customer service and reduced inventories. The planning process was used to facilitate growth and sustained profitability.[1]

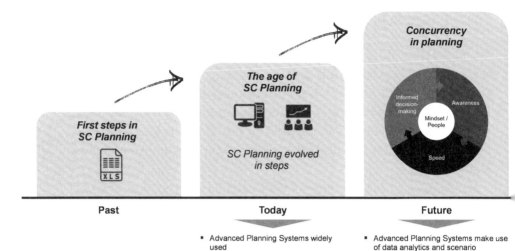

Past	Today	Future
First steps in SC Planning	**The age of SC Planning** — SC Planning evolved in steps	**Concurrency in planning**
	• Advanced Planning Systems widely used • Strong focus on improving tools, data and integration • Analytics pilots in the later phase	• Advanced Planning Systems make use of data analytics and scenario simulation • Allowing for fast, efficient and "now" based planning decisions

Figure 25: Evolution of supply chain planning

In the 90s and early 2000s many companies adopted planning philosophies and translated planning concepts from demand to supply and production planning in processes, roles and supply chain organizations. Tools were put to use to plan and optimize inventory and improve service levels.

The gap: It takes too long

However, one gap remained. Planning is and was always a strictly sequential process where demand triggered a demand review process and the finalized demand figures flowed into supply planning and later into production planning and sequencing. This led to a situation where the time from demand trigger to finalized production plan could be as long as two to three weeks. Clearly in a fast-moving world with volatile markets and high customer expectations this is too long and could lead to inadequate and incorrect plans that result in high inventory or stockouts.

The planning revolution

Future supply chain planning aims to drive the supply chain and fuel decision making through a highly responsive ("concurrent") and digitized setup that makes use of internal and external data. This then enables management decisions to be based on scenarios that drive the business. This requires an agile and reactive organization that uses data, technological capabilities and a connected ecosystem to propose solutions and scenarios anytime and anywhere. In fact, it means a demand trigger at a certain threshold will generate a supply scenario that a manager will review on his handheld device or smartphone. Concurrency breaks down the silo-based approach to planning by fusing demand, supply and production planning to a "now"-based planning concept.

There are certain key elements that are required to drive this change:

1. AWARENESS: making use of structured as well as unstructured data from known internal and external sources;
2. SPEED AND EXECUTION: from time-series forecasting based on historical data to "immediately" as things happen—the shift to "concurrent planning";
3. INFORMED DECISIONS: from human decision proposals to immediate and tool-based proposed scenarios, including probabilities and recommendations;

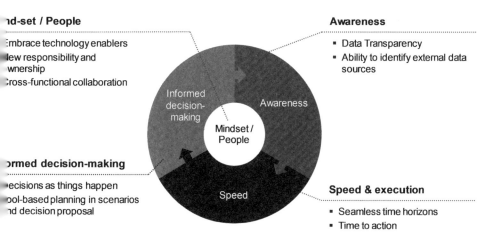

Figure 26: Key elements of the planning concept

4. **MINDSET AND PEOPLE:** steps have to be taken so that the technologies are embraced by the people supposed to use them and aligned with the organizational setup since there will be changes to the way people work.

Awareness

The revolution in planning will be driven by awareness. This stems from the ability to identify the right internal and external data sources and then use this data to connect the dots. For example, future supply chains will use IoT data from sensors in tools, goods and machines to create networks everywhere, and automate anything. The data will be stored in the cloud so it's readily accessible.

The graphic below illustrates an example of potential data sources that should be considered to address Supply Chain Planning improvements.

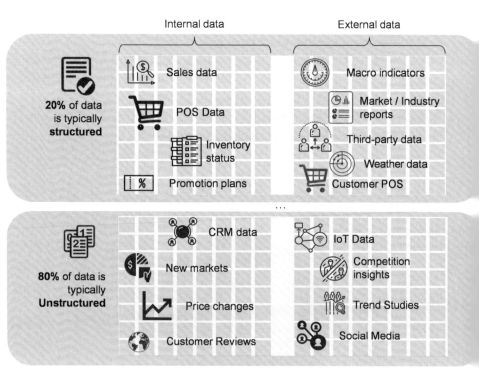

Figure 27: Classification of data sources (non-exhaustive)

Planning must take into account all of the demand data being generated outside of corporate boundaries. The key lies in finding this data, analyzing and understanding it to turn it into an advantage for the business. Advanced Analytics will be the most influential technology as far as the changing role of planners is concerned.

The future focus will be on providing the correct input data sources and handling exceptions, such as product introductions, because algorithms perform worse when there is an unexpected change.

In the future, planners will help data scientists to establish the right parameters that lead to alerts, and by doing so, they will help to automate processes and decision-making planning systems. Compared to the current state of affairs, multiple input sources will be combined and assessed to form a better basis for anticipating future demand, trends, and exceptions.

This will require a shift of skills from those currently working as demand planners from being purely concerned with demand planning via the analysis of historic data to a more varied role that also requires the skill to identify the right external data sources to improve future plans (see Chapter 4.1 for more details).

Speed and execution (concurrency)

The focus of demand planning will shift from monthly rolling forecasting to a future that is based on what just happened hours or days ago as opposed to what happened in the last year or before.

To arrive at seamless, or concurrent, time horizons data silos between different functions in the company should be removed. Then there should be no differentiation between short-, mid-, and long-term planning within the different functions so there is a combination of information from several input sources that is then used to generate a single planning solution.

A key task is to establish a link between short-term operational, day-to-day planning, mid-term financial planning, and long-term strategic planning. In this way, it will be possible to generate a more robust plan.

Instead of being a distinct process, planning will become a continuous process that can react dynamically to changing requirements or constraints such as real-time production capacity feedback from machinery. New forecasts will be produced very quickly because information availability increases by the second in a world where everything is connected. As a result, latency issues associated with traditional time-series forecasting methods, which assume that history will repeat itself over long periods of time, will be overcome.

Furthermore, the combination of analytics and AI will push supply chain planning to new levels. For supply chain planners, this means their roles will change from working in sequential manual activities using spreadsheets, to more value-added, strategic and data-driven scenario planning activities for evaluation by management.

All this adds up to forecast proposals that are purely system driven, but importantly, they should always be seen as proposals. A review cycle, or a focus from planners on specific segments that don't achieve high accuracy levels, will still be required and this in turn will further lift overall planning accuracy. This in turn will lead to better customer service levels, improved inventory management, more cost-efficient supply chain management, and is overall what's necessary to steer the business into the future.

Informed decision-making (scenarios)

Decisions will be based on better information as there will be a change from proposals generated by planners to scenario-based proposals generated by digital tools.

The traditional planning approach is based on a preparation phase to arrive at decision proposals that are prepared and evaluated by experts. In this traditional preparation phase data is collected, evaluated, and proposals are prepared manually. With advances in digital tools, it is now possible to have a faster and more reactive approach. Thinking in scenarios then becomes a feasible option, where these scenarios and their associated probabilities are generated by the system.

Smaller issues in the supply chain will be solved without human intervention and directly proposed by systems that incorporate self-learning algorithms (as proposed by tools like "Aera Technologies" or "Elementum" for example). At most, humans will only be required to confirm these machine-generated proposals.

Over time, AI will be used to propose decisions based on evaluated scenarios. This will further improve predictions based on the wealth of data collected from all participants in the network, as well as user mapping. This information will then be used to provide prescriptive solutions and automated responses and form a self-organized supply chain.

This will relieve managers from the effort of preparation and evaluation so they can focus their time and energies on key aspects of running and steering the supply chain.

Mindset and People

People play a vital role in every transformational process. Although the planning revolution has been triggered by technology, it needs to be adopted by people if it is to be successful. Section 4 of this book looks specifically at cultural transformation, or changing the mindset of employees, as the most important lever for successful digitization.

The impact on planning functions

Planners can be found across the supply chain in a number of different functions, including demand planning, inventory planning, supply planning, production planning, transport planning or order management. They typically account for one third of administrative roles in supply chain management.[2]

It's helpful to take a look in more detail at the planning process in some of these different functions.

Demand planning

Up to now, demand planners have focused on managing the demand planning process, reviewing past sales months, identifying best-fit statistical models and managing the review process with experts from sales to enrich forecasts based on market intelligence. The goal was to achieve a best-fit forecast based on internal historical data as well as sales and product know-how.

Analytics-based planning will change the way that planners work. In the future, planners will focus much more on providing the right internal and external data to enrich forecasts and enable algorithms to produce the best-fit forecasts. The role planners had in the past were resource intensive but the planners of the future will have fewer and more focused tasks and be more like data scientists or data scouts. We will elaborate on this in the following sections.

Demand planners will be much more focused on planning new product introductions. The actual analytics service itself can be run as a "black box" or even be outsourced. The advantage of an outsourced service is that it means there will be no need to keep these highly skilled individuals in house since it may be hard to keep them busy in anything other than a large business.

Based on the performance of the first pilots, solutions that come from analytics tools will gain the trust and commitment of the planner over time as the pilot projects begin to offer proof of reliability and accuracy. Even exception-based planning will be reduced with the continuous rise of AI, where the machine learns how to address certain exception cases based on past experiences.

Improve predictions

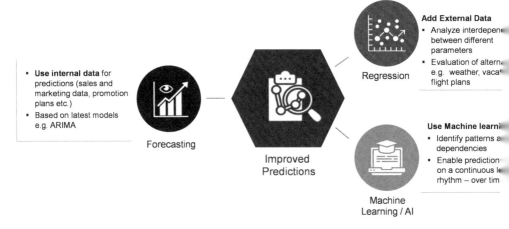

Figure 28: Generating Insights to improve Predictive Analytics

Supply planning

Traditionally, supply planners have the role of defining production plans that meet demand requirements while optimizing customer service levels, supply chain costs and inventories, a role that entails planning, re-planning and assessing planning options. This is mostly done manually and by experts, and if advanced planning solutions are available, they are supported by algorithms and optimizers to generate the plans.

The future supply planner will generate an end-to-end view in a highly responsive supply chain using advanced scenario planning tools. These tools used, will be based on machine learning and continuously optimized algorithms, and will balance demand and supply instead of creating solely feasible scenarios. The idea is not to review every scenario or exception, but to focus on the big shots and let the tool, based on its learning algorithms, select the best-fit options for minor or normal day-to-day issues and execute them automatically, although there will still be a manual overrule option.

Real-time data and constant capacity and inventory constraints will further ensure that all relevant information needed for decision making is up-to-date.

The tasks of the supply planner will be to shift to configuration ·of parameters instead of planning to arrive at scenarios.

"The dilemma for many supply planning leaders is that they have to rely on out-of-date data to predict the future, which tends to degrade the quality of the planning decisions."[3]

What is required to achive this step into the future?

In essence, the focus is not so much on reducing planning costs, reducing the number of planners or even on delivering round-the-clock support, but on providing competitive advantages by improving customer focused KPIs such as service levels, shortening lead times at competitive prices, as well as creating more time for value-added tasks by planning staff.

To generate this leap in efficiency and speed at the same time it is necessary to combine a number of capabilities in supply chain planning, as shown in the diagram below.

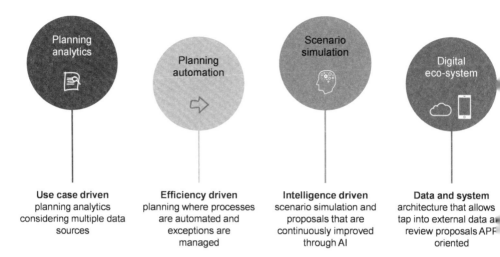

Planning analytics	Planning automation	Scenario simulation	Digital eco-system
Use case driven planning analytics considering multiple data sources	**Efficiency driven** planning where processes are automated and exceptions are managed	**Intelligence driven** scenario simulation and proposals that are continuously improved through AI	**Data and system** architecture that allows tap into external data a review proposals APP oriented

Figure 29: Future digital capabilities in supply chain planning

PLANNING ANALYTICS is Advanced Analytics applied to planning. Its huge potential was discussed in Chapter 2.2 and also in case studies in this chapter. The basis of this is its ability to consider internal and external data sources for demand or transportation planning, and also to consider analytics capabilities in production planning.

PLANNING AUTOMATION drives and supports speed but processes need to be integrated and automated in order to make concurrent planning a reality. Tool providers are supporting this step with ready-to-use or configure-to-use systems, depending on the specific business needs.

SCENARIO SIMULATION and proposals that are continuously improved through AI.

DIGITAL ECOSYSTEM, such as mobile connectivity, is the architecture that allows access to external data and review proposals that are APP-oriented.

The combination of these elements paired with adapted roles and organizational design will bring improved plans that drive the supply chain and the ability of many people to simultaneously review scenario plans across different time horizons at different levels of detail, comment on them, and achieve the goal of a fast-paced and reactive supply chain. Ultimately, scenario simulations will lead to a self-driven supply chain based on AI where a magnitude of decisions are based on past learning, limiting the need for human interventions to bigger exceptions.

To re-state what was said at the beginning of this chapter, precise predictions are the currency of the future. It is where we move from a plan created once a month to a plan that is updated continuously based on the latest internal and external data and information so that more precise and carefully evaluated decisions can be made.

How will planning organizations have to change?

The operative mode of planners will change, and a clear shift of skills will be required. Compared to what is currently done, multiple input sources can be combined and assessed to form a better basis for anticipating future demands, trends and exceptions. The skill set of current planners, that generally involves networking, collecting internal information from the likes of sales people in the case of demand planning, and savvy statistical modeling, will have to change to match the changing nature of the job they do. Existing roles may even be split into several dedicated roles, as highlighted below (see Chapter 4.1. on specific supply chain roles in the future).

- DATA SCOUTS are able to identify and correlate external data sources and transfer them into their own systems where they can be used in analytics and machine learning processes.
- DATA SCIENTISTS are able to manage and challenge multiple input sources and assess where and how to build correlations to impact demand. Data scientists need to be up-to-date with the latest statistical methods (such as Python (!), and R-Library developments) and analytics methods and tools. In addition, the experience to identify correlation and patterns will be a necessary skill for planners so they can build correlations and further improve forecasts. A certain combination of data know-how and business acumen will improve their ability to make up correlations.
- FORECASTING LIBRARY SPECIALIST run statistical predictions based on the latest statistical engines and developments. He is always alert to new developments and compares best methods including for example the R-Library (an open source library) that includes ARIMA and other models for forecasting. He works closely with the Data Scout to manage and

improve forecasts based on best-fit correlations with external or internal data sources.

- **UNIVERSAL SUPPLY CHAIN NETWORK PLANNERS** will be needed to help data scientists to identify and establish the right parameters and alerts to automate processes and decision-making planning systems. They have the ability to work in an orchestrated manner with machine-based processes to optimize overall performance.
- **SCENARIO EXCEPTION SPECIALIST** identifies disruptions of supply network and evaluates these. Scenario creation with drivers for business decisions and risk. Evaluation of scenarios and their probability.

It is only right at this point to ask the question, what will happen to the traditional demand planner? Human activities in planning will shift to more focused and different tasks such as different new product introductions, specific out-of-the-norm promotions, and error-driven or exception-driven adjustments.

Planning organizations will be impacted. For example, a previously de-central demand planning setup will change to a centralized, data science-driven planning setup supported by selected external knowledge bases. There will be less need to rely on untrustworthy sources for planning input and market intelligence, tasks that can be fulfilled by sales people in one scenario, or by the people who were previously demand planners who will have now taken on additional roles in the supply chain. However these roles may vary and be an aggregation of a data scout in one country, a data scientist in another, and a person moving to production elsewhere.

It is almost certain that analytics and AI will create new jobs for the planning entities in the future. The goods news for B2B project businesses or make-to-order businesses that did not focus so much on planning in the past is that it will become a real option. It will be centralized and add value with limited effort, yet its output will be highly relevant to planning performance and its accuracy will help to steer the business in the right direction.

Lessons learned from supply chain leaders

1. UNDERSTANDING DATA IS THE KEY TO WINNING IN THIS GAME! Data that is sorted into external and internal sources, and unstructured and structured data, will support planning outcomes and the ability to build meaningful correlations.
2. PILOT PROJECTS CAN BE RUN IN A FAIRLY SHORT-TIME FRAME. Use experts and data scientists who bring experience in this area. The recommendation is to go for it, fail fast but take what you learn and re-align for a winning setup.
3. DATA AND RESULTS WILL SOMETIMES SEEM "STRANGE" and hard to interpret, since machine learning identifies patterns that you may not recognize or have thought of before. So a certain degree of trust will be required in supply chain planning—this may take time.
4. COMPARE HUMANS TO MACHINES in a dry run. As a starting pilot, act as if you are three months back in time and create a plan for the supply chain, then compare the actual human-generated forecast data to that produced by the technology and challenge the results.
5. Don't underestimate the CHANGE MANAGEMENT involved in this process especially with people that are more traditional since the combination of analytics and AI is a disruption. This is especially true if you leapfrogged from Excel to the most advanced digital methods.
6. As in every transformation, SENIOR MANAGEMENT SUPPORT is essential to making this a success.
7. NEW PERFORMANCE MANAGEMENT will be necessary within a new supply planning process. You will need to move away from traditional forecast accuracy only benchmarking to "forecastability" measurement, since the higher your forecastability quota the better will be your plans and the more you will be able to rely on digital solutions in supply chain planning. KPIs for the rate of external data used will be essential to further improve planning.

Roadmap to success

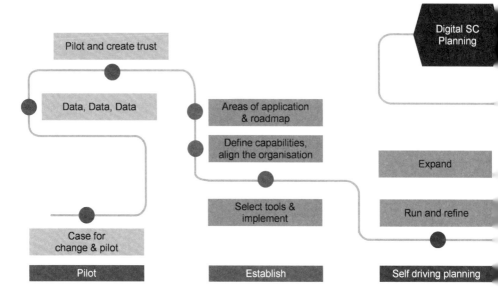

Figure 30: The roadmap to success of digital supply chain planning

STEP 1: CREATE A CASE FOR CHANGE

- Understand where the pain points are in your current supply chain planning setup.
- Where are customers impacted by missing or late goods, or where are inventories high?

STEP 2: DATA, DATA, DATA

- Information and data is the key to building analytics and AI-based pilots.
- Make sure you have access to this data, and you have structured and set up the data so it can be processed.
- Without this, the recipe for digital supply chain planning will be missing the fuel to work. This fuel includes both internal but also external data sources.

STEP 3: PILOT & CREATE TRUST

- A pilot only creates trust if it is meaningful, sizeable and creates value.
- Using the analogy of a pie, make sure your pilot design does not involve too small a slice, since digital analytics solutions are able to run sizeable slices of the pie.
- Test planning scenarios with different dimensions:
  - time series driven from daily, weekly, to monthly or quarterly plans;
  - based on internal data only;
  - adding external data and correlation analysis or machine learning.
- Act as if it is three months back in time and then create the forecast for the coming month. At the same time create plans to predict reality. In this way you can fine-tune your algorithms in the short term but also create trust by running real predictions—where accuracy shows over time.

STEP 4: AREAS OF APPLICATION & ROADMAP

There are several routes that can be taken from pilot to wider application. Obviously the first step is to extend the pilot scope to other areas within the domain. But beside this, the scope can also be extended to other areas of application in logistics, transportation, demand or supply planning or inventory management.

STEP 5: DEFINE CAPABILITIES, ALIGN THE ORGANIZATION

New and revised capabilities will be required to leverage digital solutions and their capabilities. As outlined previously, a fundamental shift in competencies may be required.

STEP 6: SELECT TOOLS AND IMPLEMENT THEM

This is a key question—which tools should be run? There is a multitude of supply chain planning solutions on the market so it is simply not possible to elaborate on them here. We at h&z have supported numerous selection processes in this space. Our key takeaway and recommendation is to go beyond pure PowerPoint and the demo presentations offered by vendors and move into demo sessions based on your own data—only then will you see relevant results and understand how they may relate to your own business. Another option is to outsource Advanced Analytics services. This limits the investment you'd need in resources, training and the software, and obviously the ramp up in this case is much faster. However, do not underestimate the learning curve required to trust plans generated by machines.

STEPS 7/8: RUN, REFINE AND EXPAND

Once launched, results that were first piloted will improve over time. Then add more external data and more intelligent algorithms and watch while trust in the system grows. Once you get to this stage, expand planning analytics to other segments.

Chapter 3.3
Logistics today and tomorrow
Thomas Tapp

Introduction

The logistics sector has grown significantly in importance in recent years. In Germany, for example, the logistics industry grew by 3% annually from €154bn in 2000 to €279bn in 2019, while across Europe it grew by 2% annually from €950bn in 2008 to €1.12bn in 2018.[1]

Clearly the logistics sector is in good shape, but it nevertheless faces certain challenges if it is to master the increasingly complex flows of goods, to improve efficiency while maintaining flexibility and to meet increasingly demanding as well as specific customer requirements while maintaining quality.

As an operational discipline, logistics has become an important competitive differentiator. In recent years, issues such as process optimization, automation and sustainability (green logistics) have been of primary importance. Today, it's digitalization.[2]

Advantages and limits of digitalization

The digitalization of logistics offers numerous advantages. Many logistics service providers have already been able to significantly reduce personnel costs in their warehouses or in transport logistics by automating standard processes.

Most companies combine digitalization with the goal of higher delivery reliability. To this end, digitalization offers various levers such as greater transparency, enhanced predictability, improved planning, effective risk management, and more tailored services. Furthermore, today's IT enables companies to be more flexible, responsive and agile in their processes and thus react faster and more specifically to customer and market requirements.

Another advantage of digitalization is better control and mitigation of the complexity of the logistics processes. Here, digitalization improves networking and comprehensive automation. It leads to enhanced transparency and enables those involved in a supply chain to collaborate more smoothly. By connecting the many participants and company-wide IT-based collaboration, data becomes comprehensively available to any party involved. On this basis, additional information and insights are created, such as being able to assess risks in the supply chain at an early stage. The improved, deep knowledge of the entire process constitutes an important prerequisite for developing further innovative ideas.

Further advantages, such as improved efficiency, error prevention, risk mitigation, automation, and solid decision-making bases through comprehensive information, contribute to cost reduction. At the same time, new services such as data analysis and interpretation lead to higher customer satisfaction. On this basis, new business fields and sales potentials can be created.

Experience shows, however, that some of the systems are not yet fully developed and cause errors. The troubleshooting that follows can override the savings that were supposed to be inherent in using the system in the first place.

Today, every malfunction in the complex logistics chain causes great damage as soon as it occurs. Therefore, systems must be designed redundantly, robust and carefully protected from external influences. When deciding whether and to what extent such precautionary measures should be taken, reliability and efficiency of the logistics chain must be reconciled.

New business models and value-added services

According to industry experts of the DSLV (Bundesverband Spedition und Logistik e. V.), the digitalization of logistics will contribute significantly to the development of innovative business models. We are already seeing logistics service providers offering the management of data and documents along the logistics chain in addition to freight transport or warehousing and handling services.

Value-added services associated with this can include, for example, the targeted evaluation of data and the provision of recommendations for action planning, the efficient use of resources, the bundling of transports, the networking of logistics chains or the improvement of logistics performance indicators for the respective customers. The service provider is able to offer the experience and data evaluations of a large number of customers. The shippers can make their data available to the service providers and thus benefit from the networks in return.

The new digital business models should be designed to fully exploit the potential of digitalization in combination with powerful IT. Such services help reduce complexity with automated processes that enable end-to-end visibility, transparency and collaboration. For example, they can contribute to increasing efficiency by reducing errors or avoiding risks through early detection and avoiding waste by making better use of existing logistics capacities.[3]

The digital business models also increase the flexibility of the supply chain by means such as diverting shipments, later collection, or using different transportation modes.

Some of these new business models and value-added services are described in the following section.

Business models with value-added services

"In a digital supply chain various digital elements will replace analog elements [...]. However, everyone is aware that logistics is not feasible without sensible digital support and companies can only be successful in the future if they take this into account."

Peter Dressler, Senior Director Logistics, Infineon

Blockchain

The use of blockchain technology is beneficial in logistics and is expected to reduce transport related costs.

Firstly, it helps to verify the origin of shipped parts and can record the motion of all shipments. The origin and transport sequence of every shipment can be tracked and traced via publicly distributed ledgers. These ledgers provide information to all actors in a transport sequence and help to establish transparency (see Chapter 2.1 for a more detailed overview of blockchain).

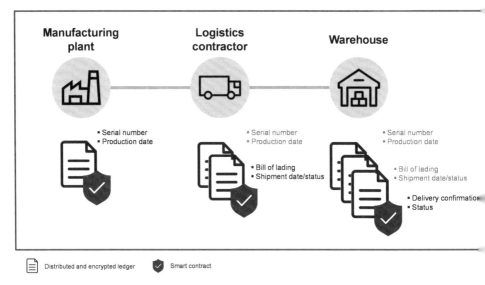

Figure 31: Simplified Blockchain in logistics

Secondly, the possibility to have blockchain-backed smart contracts helps to save costs by making brokerages, lawyers and other third parties unnecessary. Smart contracts can orchestrate shipment flows based on self-executing contracts between anonymous parties with terms that have been codified in the ledgers. The agreements and the necessary code are also saved in the distributed ledger that is encrypted but shared between all participants in the decentralized logistics chain. Smart contracts make central entities holding the authority over a transaction unnecessary and external enforcement mechanisms become redundant. All transactions are transparent and traceable and cannot be reversed.[4]

Automatic storage systems and autonomous warehouses

Lineage Logistics, a company operating in the food industry, is making full use of digital technologies to improve its business.

For example, Lineage Logistics has used AI to create an intelligent warehouse management system aimed at optimizing inventories. The system uses smart pallet placement as part of a process to forecast when orders will arrive and leave a warehouse where the replacement of pallets can be optimized as a result of the improved forecasting. This has increased Lineage Logistics' efficiency by 20%.

Another Lineage Logistics example from 2018 is that their data scientists and engineers teamed up and secured a patent for an algorithm to optimize the storage of pallets. The algorithm uses data from lidar scans of the 162 existing buildings and calculated the most space-efficient way to store the products. As a result, Lineage generated a total of approximately 74,000 m² additional storage.[5]

It is in the nature of food logistics that the associated energy costs for cooling are very high, so Lineage decided to use digital technology to tackle this problem. They installed thousands of IoT sensors to optimize temperatures in their warehouses over the course of the day. They did this by training an AI algorithm with the sensor data. Over a period of three years, the company has reduced energy consumption in its warehouses by 34%, which equates to approximately US$4m per year.[6] Visibility of goods with clear tracking is crucial for logistic functions. Digital solutions support tracking of goods as well as location management. Location management via RFID is already well established. Tracking of goods, that cannot be marked with RFID tags is moving into the focus for digital solution. One example is the tracking of hot steel slaps after casting. Warehouses equipped with 3D cameras allow full visibility of objects that are stored or move into and out of the warehouse. Digital solution scans every slap with their specific dimension and track their position. Allocation to production and logistic orders enable management of every piece.

Digital solutions will provide necessary transparency. Management has to define the level of solution coverage as well as the added value. Local solutions to bridge information islands are in focus. Often it is not necessary to get transparency into every area.

"Track and trace technology can be a double-edged sword. If you announce that the goods will be there tomorrow at a certain time, then why do we still need to track the shipment? I believe today 95–96% of our tracking data are not viewed. This begs the question, is it not better to call the customer in person in the few cases where a shipment will not arrive on time? Doing this has the added benefit of more personal customer service. But this will change a lot in the future and tracking platforms and IoT solutions will become more standard in logistics. On the cost side, you would probably have about ten people sitting in the head office calling customers, but you would have saved the costs of the tracking equipment."

Erik Wirsing, Vice President Global Innovation, DB Schenker

Autonomous vehicles

Details about the importance of autonomous vehicles as a part of the transformation of supply chain management were presented in Chapter 2.1. However, it is worth recapping briefly here as they will play a vital future role in logistics of the future.

Autonomous driverless vehicles have been in use for a long time in the field of internal logistics and have proven themselves in many areas. Prominent examples are the fully automated container terminals, which are already successfully operating in numerous ports around the world. Further examples with the use of Automated Guided Vehicles (AGVs) are automated milk runs in production supply or automatic storage and retrieval processes in large warehouses, where the AGVs organize themselves according to cost and efficiency criteria and independently select and execute the respective transport orders.

We will also see fleets of autonomous trucks with only one human operative driving in platoon style (one behind the other—see Chapter 2.1) on Europe's roads by 2025.

As different as the above examples may be, they all have some basic features in common:

- The autonomously running processes are highly standardized
- The processes run in a clearly defined environment

- The underlying data meets the highest quality requirements in terms of completeness, correctness and integrity
- Humans are not obsolete, but exercise control functions and intervene when necessary
- The qualification requirements for the personnel employed are significantly higher than is usual for conventional transport processes

Beside autonomous driving automation can provide optimal support for forklift drivers and thus improve safety as well as efficiency. One example for such a digital solution is obstacle detection (e.g. people) and coalition avoidance in warehouses. In addition to the increased safety of the employees, it was shown that the speed of the forklifts could be increased by 15%. Turn of investment of that kind of support functions is relatively short and serves sustainable people management.

Geofencing or geo-localization in logistics

Anyone who orders a taxi or a pizza with the help of their smartphone can track the current location of the vehicle in real time and predict the arrival time with a high degree of accuracy. This technology, which is already widely used in the B2C sector, but it has clear applications in B2B logistics (see also Chapter 2.1) including an early warning system and theft protection in fleet management. However, technologies have also opened up many new application areas.

Time-window delivery and same day delivery are hot topics, especially when it comes to the problem of the last mile. An example of how this is being tackled is Amazon's patented Anticipatory Shipping. It uses machine learning to analyze extensive internal data, including surfing and ordering behavior, personal wish lists, personal customer data, personal Internet information, demographic data, and customers' retail environments, to predict at which location which products are ordered and at which time. Amazon is thus able to optimize the shipment of goods and has cut delivery times by up to two hours, benefits that are passed on directly to consumers.

Future role of IT in Logistics

As in any other business area, the role of IT for logistics has been widened significantly in the past and will grow evermore quickly in the upcoming years. The importance of IT for the logistics industry, and the companies' logistics departments will become even more important than it is today. At the same time, IT is the driver for completely new innovative value-added solutions (such as those highlighted above) for both external customers and internal users and offers tools and applications for process optimization regarding efficiency, transparency, and reliability.

The success of logistics in the value chains of the future depends more than ever on how well processes are digitalized, how closely they are networked and how smoothly organizational units work together. The biggest challenges to the digitalization of logistics come in the form of integrating all parties involved in a value chain and mapping the entire enterprise-wide business processes in fully integrated IT workflows.

Logistics operators should embrace IT, and its future leading role in the sector because it can add substantially to competitiveness. Clever and comprehensive use of IT offers numerous opportunities to provide innovative logistics services and value-added services that can be quickly, reliably and cost-effectively tailored to the needs of individual customers.

The examples below highlight the increasing role of IT in logistics.

Gains in transparency

The ability to process and evaluate mass data in the shortest possible time and the automatic recognition of recurring patterns using learning algorithms make it possible to obtain new information from data that has been collected from a variety of sources. This is achieved above all through targeted consolidation and analysis of previously unrelated data. This makes it possible, for example, to identify imminent disruptions in the logistics chain at an early stage and take appropriate measures in good time. This contributes significantly to the consistency of the supply chain risk management.

Gains in reliability

Using telematics, transponders, RFID chips and sensors, it is possible to compare local reality and process progress better and faster with the planning and control level. This avoids errors, rectifies malfunctions more quickly and draws the right conclusions from the past.

This successively improves the quality of the planning and execution (such as delivery reliability, and adherence to delivery dates) of the logistics processes, which in turn leads to an increase in robustness and reliability of logistics processes.

Gains in efficiency

At the same time, logistics provides numerous control and decision-relevant data and information in real time. This means, for example, that transport and storage capacities can be better utilized, routes better planned, disturbances reacted to more quickly and errors corrected immediately. By automating standardized processes, these are significantly accelerated and can be managed with fewer resources. In addition, automated processes run with fewer errors, and the course and progress of the process can be better monitored and controlled.

Overall, there is a significant reduction in waste of time and resources.

Lessons for Implementation

Starting a project to digitalize logistics need not be a daunting prospect. There are some key considerations that will help the success of the project.

"The main hindrances we faced in our early attempts at digitalization were in the interactions with our customers. In some cases, IT projects that had been set up could not be carried out because of budget restrictions or because the resources we needed weren't available."

Roland Becker, Managing Director, GLX Logistics

Clear objectives

The decision to digitalize processes, offer digital solutions to customers or embark on a completely new business model is an important strategic decision for any organization and must be carefully prepared.

First, it is vital to have clear objectives for the digitalization process. Digitalization for the sake of it is to be avoided at all costs.

As the starting point of the digital transformation, define what is to be digitalized, with which target and when.

Step-by-step approach

Digitalization projects are very complex, especially when a large number of processes in the company have to be changed. If too many changes are needed at once, there is a risk that the entire organization will be overwhelmed which could lead to the project being scrapped or at least delayed. The best approach is to start small but take quick, successive steps, making sure each step is complete before moving on to the next.

Comprehensive implementation

Developing a good idea is the first step. But implementing it consistently is often difficult. This is especially true for completely new areas such as digitalization.

Against the backdrop of ever faster digitalization, existing technological gaps in a company can grow just as rapidly. This can lead to considerable competitive disadvantages, so that the gap can no longer be closed.

Therefore, the wide range of technological possibilities offered by digitalization should be fully exploited. Consequently, the aim should be to digitalize the process by the integration of IT system along the supply chain. Systems like ERP, MES or CRM system can be used to close the current gaps in the process.

Adapt organization

When undergoing a digital transformation, it might be necessary to break up existing organizational units in order to create stronger cooperation between departments and companies. However, digitalization makes everything faster so there could be increased decision-making pressure, making the working environment more unpredictable. This requires a great deal of tact and sensitivity on the part of managers and, at the same time, the ability and willingness of employees to assume responsibility.

One approach is to create a "digitalization community" within the company, where each department appoints a digitalization officer to work in an agile corporate team.

Improve data quality

Data is the most important asset in digitalization. New business areas or services such as analytics are based on data that enables logistics companies to manage the supply chain more reliably and efficiently. The most important prerequisites are correct, complete and validated basic data. This is currently one of the biggest obstacles for many companies. There is a chance that existing data, such as material master data, status information and order data, is often incomplete, contradictory and incorrect and thus becomes ineffective. Often data is not available quickly at the push of a button because it is stored in different media or interfaces which are not suitable for data exchange.

Improved data quality and data management are prerequisites to digitalization.

Involve employees

"I think that the employee who carries out manual work today will be the supervisor of these activities tomorrow, or the controller who does the fine-tuning to ensure quality. The new roles will depend on observing, steering, controlling and maintaining instead of executing."

Erik Wirsing, Vice President Global Innovation, DB Schenker

A recurring theme throughout this book is that digital transformation has a cultural, human as well as a technological dimension. If your people are not prepared for the changes digitalization will bring, then even with the best technology in the world the process will fail (see Chapter 4.2).

In brief, employees must be informed about digitalization projects and their goals in a timely and comprehensive manner. This increases the acceptance of the projects and helps to reduce the reservations and fears of the employees. It is the employees and their commitment that determine the success of digitalization. When there is resistance, it is important for all staff to undergo training programs to help change the current culture and foster a digital mindset.

It is also vital that employees are equipped with the right skills and knowledge to work effectively with the new processes digitalization brings. This could again involve training or bringing in new people.

Share data

An important prerequisite for the success of the digital transformation is the willingness to share the data. Digitalization can only be successful when common standards are developed across the logistics industry. This requires mutual trust and cooperation. Companies that want to gain from digitalization therefore must share data in order to profit from those who analyze and process it.

Practitioners' View (Interviews)

Digitalization of logistics at Elflein Spedition und Transport GmbH

Expert interview with Hartwig Meinen, Managing Director Logistics, Elflein Spedition & Transport GmbH

For Hartwig Meinen, Managing Director Logistics at Elflein Spedition & Transport GmbH, it will also be unavoidable for medium-sized logistics service providers in a few years to have completed the digitalization of logistics in order to be able to assert themselves on the market.

In his opinion, digitalization is a future trend that can be implemented over a longer period of time in an evolutionary process.

How has digitalization affected your business environment?

Digitalization affects the business environment because it's changing the expectations of our customers. Our customers in the transport segment are demanding evermore precise information about the estimated time of arrival of their deliveries. They also want to be able to track online exactly where their shipments are at a specific point of time. Our customers in the automotive and food retail industries expect to be proactively informed of disruptions and other events.

Digitalization is affecting contract logistics in a similar way. Our customers expect full transparency about material flows in the warehouse as well as in production. They expect complete transparency about automatic material call-offs. They also expect warehouse management to be highly efficient.

Do you think digitalization is vital for the survival of logistics service providers?

Digitalization cannot be avoided. It's crucial for medium-sized logistics service providers and they'll have to undergo digitalization if they want to remain competitive.

Digitalization is an evolutionary process. The solutions and transformation activities that are necessary can be implemented over an extended period of time.

How have you prepared your company and yourself for digitalization?

Digitalization is given a high priority in our company. As of this year, we created a position for a digitalization manager. The digitalization manager will initially align our processes with the requirements of digitalized logistics and then the system landscape will be standardized. We're doing this because we want to ensure that we remain on top of our customers constantly changing requirements.

What digital solutions do you already offer your customers today?
Geolocating and geofencing have enabled our customers to see exactly where each trailer is at any given moment. The dispositioning tool sends an immediate message to our customers about any delays or malfunctions. It means we can react flexibly and immediately to unforeseen events.

In the contract logistics segment, we are increasingly focusing on driverless systems, which are replacing the classic route train.

Where do you see the greatest potential for digitalizing logistics?
There is huge potential for using digitalization in logistics because it enables companies to make better use of their resources, to use them more efficiently and avoid waste. This will lead to an optimal use of transport and storage capacities. For example, empty runs can be avoided and return freight can be better planned and more targeted.

In your opinion, what are the success factors for digitalizing logistics?
A success factor for a digitalization project is the way it's executed. It should be carried out quickly so you don't lose traction. However, attempts to implement digitalization projects as a "big bang" will be too much for the organization and its employees.

It's vital to have an experienced project manager or program manager to plan and manage digitalization projects. The respective project manager might have to be brought into the company from outside and should ideally have a track record of successfully implementing digitalization projects in other companies.

It's also a prerequisite and a crucial success measure of any digitalization project that it yields a return on investment in under two-and-a-half years, even for the more complex projects.

Chapter 3.4
Supply Chain Visibility: Connecting the dots
Thomas Mrozek

Case Study: How visibility solves headphone envy

Just imagine for a moment that you want a new pair of headphones. Perhaps a colleague of yours came into the office with a new pair that you secretly like and it's prompted you to get a pair just like them, or maybe something even better. Even though this is a spontaneous, last-minute decision, the process of ordering your new headphones could not be easier or more transparent.

You take out your smartphone, go to Amazon, and although there's a huge selection of headphones available you already know roughly what you want and quickly narrow your search until you find exactly the pair you're looking for. You're then just two clicks away from completing the order, and having done so, you almost immediately receive an email from Amazon confirming the order and the delivery time and place for the following day.

B2C has it all—but why?

The entire process, from decision making to purchase, takes just a few minutes, even if you spend time reading a few reviews of different models. There's no time wasted by being presented with suggested items that aren't available but rather a range of options that are immediately available. Your time isn't wasted by being presented with unavailable items because the most likely outcome of this is a lost sale. Everything about the process—from the range of items you'd be presented with, comparisons with similar products, to the transparent costs and delivery options—was designed to get you to make a purchase.

Why does it seem so easy in the B2C sector when this isn't always the case in B2B transactions? Why can't you use your smartphone in a production facility to order the best raw material when you need it, confident that it will arrive on time and in full? In our perspective there are differences in the way B2B and B2C companies work, manage their supply chains and satisfy customer needs. Historically, supply chain professionals expected differences between customer and consumer behaviors and expectations. Today we note that this expectation gap is closing quickly.

This is hardly surprising given that the B2B buyer is a consumer too. Why should he or she accept that the nature of the treatment they receive, and the process involved in making a purchase on behalf of the company they work for, should be any different to buying a pair of headphones or any other consumer item for themselves?

On the contrary, it's logical to expect at least the same if not better service when you're placing an order for €20m rather than a comparatively small amount for a pair of headphones.

Background: Supply chain visibility isn't new, but it's changing

While the idea of supply chain visibility (SCV) isn't new, the understanding and use cases have seen changes over the years. For example, the supply chain is an integrated network of partners and not a controlled entity contained within the four walls of a warehouse. It's a much more complex process today, involving a network of resources scattered across multiple facilities and locations all over the world (see Figure 32). This complexity obviously makes visibility more challenging and some years ago the idea of full supply chain visibility may have looked like a distant dream. But this is changing and most companies are pursuing some degree of visibility across the supply chain to stay up to date and provide customers with a seamless experience. Maybe it is not full visibility, but it's the beginning.

Figure 32: Network of Resources

The barriers to SC visibility

Even without knowing the full range of benefits that come with supply chain visibility (which we'll explore in detail later) if you were to ask yourself as a supply chain executive whether you'd like to have better, faster and more accurate supply chain transparency, you'd answer with an emphatic "Yes." It's something we all want. Visibility initiatives can be focused on any aspect of the supply chain, from supplier compliance to customer demand sensing, but it's not that easy. There are of course numerous barriers standing in the way that make it difficult to achieve transparency along the supply chain. Let's take a look at some of them here.

Increasing complexity of supply chain management

Many organizations function globally, and this naturally makes business more complex. In many manufacturing companies, as much as 80% of its value-add is within the supplier network and may take place outside of its own four walls. There'll be different ways and means of logistics and shipping goods to its customers, and its suppliers will be both local and overseas.

Furthermore, if suppliers are located across the world it is obvious that the suppliers themselves do have suppliers, creating an N-Tier Supply Chain. This increases required links, ecosystems and data to create transparency across the full supply chain. This means data such as part numbers, drawings and specifications, sources of origin and destinations are kept not only in one system but in many, causing an issue around harmonization of data. Traditional enterprise resource planning (ERP) is not built to cope with this kind of challenge to manage so much information.

Hence, there is complete consensus that having good visibility along the supply chain is indispensable to tracking supplier network activity precisely and accomplishing short and accurate lead times to customers, but the very nature of these widespread and complex supply chains makes visibility hard to achieve.

Case study: heavy-duty problems in manufacturing

A heavy machinery manufacturing company was steadily growing. Its products were of the best quality and demand for them was high. However, the production of one machine required hundreds of parts from different suppliers scattered all over the world, with lead times from days to weeks, and in one case up to three months.

Delays in supply led to missing parts and disrupted production, which in turn affected the delivery times to customers.

The chief supply chain manager summed up the problems faced by the company: "We're able to manufacture products of the highest quality for our customers but we're unable to say where in the supply chain the product is or to ensure on-time delivery."

Unexpected demand changes of customers

Another barrier to visibility comes in the form of the greater number of choices customers have today. This is illustrated by a recent h&z study which showed that 52% of participating companies feared "unexpected demand changes" as the single biggest factor causing disruptions in the supply chain.

It stands to reason that when customers have more options, they get used to demanding shorter and more flexible lead times and in turn they're less tolerant of mistakes and late deliveries. Add into the mix the fact that modern customers expect shorter product cycle times and it becomes clear that to meet these challenges, forecasting and forward visibility are more important than ever to the success of your business.

This means that you, as the supplier, need a viable, effective supply chain with a steady and stable flow of data. A setup to provide an end-to-end view of the supply chain that leads to improved transparency on incoming supplies and allows effective control.

Accelerating market volatility and intensified response times

Nobody likes market volatility, but it's a fact of life. In the past decade market volatility within each market domain has accelerated, making the job of supply chain executives even trickier. In parallel to this, the time required to take action based upon subtle changes in the supply chain within and across domains is decreasing. This combination of **accelerated volatility** and **intensified speed of responsiveness**, along with more complex supply chains, mean executives are faced with difficult decisions on a daily basis.

Complexity of IT Systems

Information technology can help solve many problems faced by supply chain managers, but at the same time the complexity inherent in them can present new challenges. IT systems are often siloed and diverse, so rather than delivering global inventory transparency they muddy the waters. However, this transparency is key to determining whether or not there is a need to re-order or if there is a potential stock-out situation.

One answer to inventory management issues such as these is to use a cloud-based SaaS solution. The problem is, they're not yet being widely used. The share of cloud-based inventory systems increased from 12% in 2008 to 87% in 2018. However, despite being widely available, in 2018 only 39% of companies were running cloud-based solutions.[1]

The conclusion to be drawn from this is that if you want to see continued growth in your company not only will it be advantageous to invest in a cloud-based system now, it will be absolutely necessary in the future.

Compliance with regulatory requirements

Supply chain visibility tools help to keep track of the ever-changing landscape of regulations and compliance. This is especially critical for organizations that work globally when it comes to handling different trade agreements and tariffs. Additionally, supply chain visibility tools enable company leaders to better predict and respond to new regulations in their industry.[2]

The problems caused by a lack of visibility

Now that we've looked at some of the most common barriers to supply chain visibility, let's highlight some of the problems that arise because of them, beginning with some thought-provoking figures.

At a glance: the problems in figures

- 70% of firms described their supply chain as "very" or "extremely complex"
- 6% said they have "full visibility" into their entire supply chain
- 74% said they use four to five different transportation modes in their supply chain
- 81% of firms are using one-to-three KPIs to assess supply chain performance
- 84% outsource their transportation service[3]

Data silos and traditional communication

Unfortunately, problems surrounding information visibility aren't only related to external supply chain information—departmental silos remain a serious concern in many organizations. Two thirds (67%) of companies confirm information sharing between departments is a significant or very significant issue affecting their ability to achieve visibility across the supply chain. Indeed, you need only to look at the communication methods still in use across manufacturing sectors to understand why achieving accurate, up-to-date information is extremely difficult.[4]

Where are we today with system connectivity in the B2B environment?

Efforts are now three decades old; yet, as shown in Figure 33 below, the primary mechanisms are based on traditional efforts such as phone, mail and EDI for data interchange. The dependency on spreadsheets is limiting the evolution of supply chain visibility.

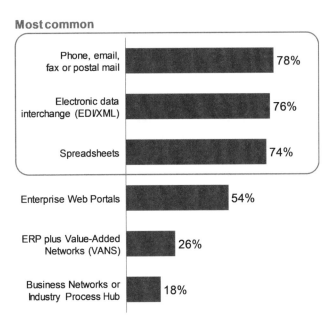

Figure 33: B2B solutions currently used[5]

One of the biggest pain points in today's supply chain is the limited ability to respond proactively to fluctuations in demand. For example, operations staff had no clue that they were not stocking adequate quantities of parts in the warehouses. This lack of information has often costly consequences such as temporarily stopped production sites, air freight express orders or delayed deliveries. To solve this problem, companies and suppliers need full visibility into all orders to react in real time to shortages or overcapacities. This would allow a supply chain manager to take action before the situation becomes critical and reduces or eliminates expedited fees.

Visibility matters

It's clear, even from these brief insights, that visibility creates benefits in terms of revenue uplift, cost reduction and optimized working capital. This is worth striving for, isn't it? If you have a better understanding of supply chain flows through the network you'll get greater visibility, and in turn this information can be used to forewarn of upcoming issues and reduce inefficiencies. There is of course an easy way out of this. You could simply reject the need for transparency and try to future-proof your supply chain by increasing your inventory, adding capacity at different locations and having multiple suppliers to call on. But what then happens to your efforts to improve the cost efficiency of your supply chain?

There are strong arguments in favor of supply chain visibility and, let's be honest, none against it. Visibility really does matter, but how do you get there? Supply chain simulation systems, supported by scenario simulation, offer the opportunity to make informed and evaluated decisions about the supply chain and where visibility is lacking or otherwise. We'll illustrate this with an example in simulation.

 SMOOTH FLIGHT SIMULATION

An Aerospace OEM wasn't sure if large orders it had placed would materialize on time or would be delivered later than anticipated. This uncertainty had a huge impact on its own supply chain, and those of its suppliers, affecting production capacity, labor levels and raw materials. Through scenario-simulating and higher visibility of the supply chain, the management team of the OEM could evaluate the impact of a large order materializing on time versus it being postponed. They could see the effects on revenue, recurring costs and working capital.

To achieve visibility, systems need to be connected because only connected systems can provide a granular view of material flows through the supply chains. This can be done by using either a platform or a cloud solution.

Data is fed into the cloud-based platform and can then be processed into advanced algorithms that provide information and data to descriptive, Predictive, and Prescriptive Analytics. The result is a "control tower" that supply chain managers can use to predict and respond to shortages, disruptions or inefficient material flows.

DEEP DIVE—SUPPLY CHAIN CONTROL TOWER

Supply chain control towers enable supply chain orchestration through increased visibility, collaboration and optimization within the entire value chain. It works as a cross-functional tool (or digital platform) empowered to monitor, analyze and take suitable actions to improve specific, predefined KPIs across the extended value chain based on three major components:

- Early 360 degree visibility (**visibility**)
  Information from across systems and processes is shared at the right time
- Collaborative responsive mechanism (**collaboration**)
  Disparate functions across the supply chain network work in harmony via workflow management capabilities, and provide the means to collaborate across multiple functional areas both within and outside the organization to effectively respond to an event
- Cognitive computing engine (**optimization**)
  Information is monitored and analyzed; analytical tools assist decision making, apply intelligence to business processes, anticipate and prioritize issues, predict disruptions, mitigate effectively, and ensure smart, autonomous decision making

As a result, control towers can represent a significant step from what companies are often accustomed to—which typically involves organizational silos and disjointed systems—to increased end-to-end visibility of real-time events, improved collaboration with external partners and internal divisions, and a flexible approach to technology applications.

"Digital supply chain control towers are becoming increasingly relevant for the larger medium-sized companies and all companies with global operations. Control towers are becoming more important as a consequence of globalization. Customers want to have the same service standards in other countries as they have, for example, in Germany. Most of the surveillance activities that need to be done could be performed manually by employees but it takes a lot of staff to do this and it's difficult to scale. There's a growing demand for control towers in the supply chain since customers are becoming more global. If you can offer your customers logistics services so they don't have to take care of that themselves, it's a big win for everyone."

Erik Wirsing, Vice President Global Innovation, DB Schenker

How visibility creates value

Supply chain visibility creates value in a number of different ways, including increased revenues, decreased operating expenses and more efficient inventory management. Exactly how is summarized below.

Top-line (revenue)

- Driven by visibility on demand, forecasts improve and result in reduced stock-out situations.
- Improved visibility helps aid supply chain planning so that shortages can be prevented.
- Scenario simulations (see above) can support decision making and optimize product supply, improve availability, and lead to better customer satisfaction, which in turn will likely boost revenue.
- Every 3% increase in forecast accuracy increased profit margins by 2%, according to previous h&z project experience.
- According to h&z project experience, improved visibility can increase revenue by 1–3% depending on the industry sector.

Bottom-line (operating expenses)

While increased visibility into the supply chain can boost revenues, a lack of visibility can result in costs along the supply chain.

- Unexpected demand changes result in more frequent changes in production campaigns, which in turn result in higher production costs and inefficiencies
- Missing raw materials may result in unplanned production downtimes meaning extra costs can be incurred for rushed orders and express deliveries. For example, as a result of the Japan earthquake and the consequent disruption to supplies, electronics parts had to be shipped by air to Germany and even by helicopter to the final production site of a company in Regensburg to prevent costly downtimes of the production lines
- There are higher logistics costs for express deliveries of incoming and outgoing goods to customers to meet promised delivery dates
- By reducing volatility, it's possible to increase capacity levels and use optimized processes. Over the year, we optimized supply chains across different industries. We analyzed the achievements, and the result is impressive: reductions of 6–18% in manufacturing, warehousing as well as distribution costs by applying these techniques.

Inventory

- Currently, the variability of supply and demand is being managed by companies building inventory buffers for raw materials, intermediates and finished products. Such a buffer is determined through analysis and the use of statistical methods to optimize inventory
- Volatility in demand and uncertainty of demand drive companies to keep stock levels higher than necessary to cover for uncertainty
- Past projects have shown that companies with a sturdy visibility on supply and demand can achieve an inventory reduction of 12–24%

A recipe for establishing SCM visibility

 In the same way that even the most complex recipes for delicious meals are broken down into a series of steps, there is also a step-by-step recipe for establishing visibility along the supply chain. This is our recipe for exactly that.

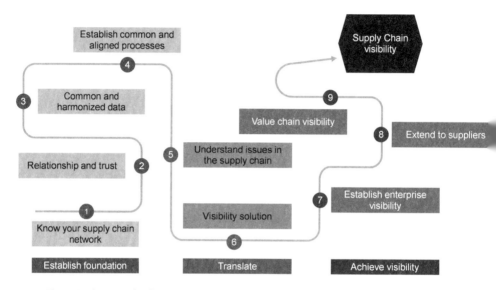

Figure 34: h&z Supply Chain visibility roadmap

STEP 1: KNOW YOUR SUPPLY CHAIN

Extend your understanding of your supply chain to key elements of your network, including suppliers and customers as well as the suppliers of your suppliers. Understand the nature of the pain points in your current network and supply chain and where they are.

Identify examples of where visibility and end-to-end views may add value and help steer the supply chain.

STEP 2: BUILD RELATIONSHIPS & TRUST

Share information across functional silos such as planning, sourcing, production, and delivery leading to additional benefits. Without this, the basic ingredients needed for visibility simply won't work in combination with each other. Share information cross-functionally within the company and with partners, providing a real end-to-end view on the supply chain. This requires trust, the essential ingredient of any good relationship, to share information for the benefit of all parties connected to the supply chain.

STEP 3: MAKE SURE YOU HAVE ALL THE MAIN INGREDIENTS
For supply chain visibility, there are two ingredients that you simply can't do without.

1. Common and harmonized data:
   - Develop specific data requirements that can be shared between partners in the supply chain to make demand planning possible.
2. Common and aligned processes:
   - Make all processes accessible for all parties to collaborate, with data sharing and planning done across all relevant functions and between companies in the supply chain.
   - Give assistance to suppliers to anticipate future demand when sales projections are coordinated with the supply chain.
   - However, this requires trust, but we've already included this.

STEP 4: UNDERSTAND THE ISSUES THAT AFFECT THE SUPPLY CHAIN
There are inevitably a number of separate issues affecting visibility along your supply chain. Choose the right order to deal with these to get the best results.

- Understand the source of each main issue.
- Address the question: What are the key areas that require improved visibility?
- Ask yourself: Do you want to start upstream with supplier visibility, since this is causing the biggest headache, or is the availability of your product to customers the key issue? Or it could be that real-time inventory visibility is the main problem since the many systems and processes involved in this are blocking your attempts at visibility.
- Know what you need to do and in what order you need to do it.

STEP 5: DELIVER A VIABLE VISIBILITY SOLUTION
There are some essential checks you can perform before getting the visibility you're aiming for.

- Ask yourself, are either your current enterprise resource planning or supply chain solutions ready to address real-time visibility?
- Larger corporations use various IT systems to coordinate and manage internal and external operations but this makes it more complicated to share data and achieve visibility. Try to avoid the use of many IT systems.
- Recent technological developments are bringing supply chain visibility within reach of even the most complicated supply chains. Use them to increase the visibility.

STEPS 5/6: ESTABLISH VISIBILITY

The last steps are to establish visibility and further fine-tune based on the learnings. Once confidence and trust are established, extending the visibility to suppliers is on the radar screen. Depending on maturity of the supply chain this may be a two-to-three-year journey.

Tips

Before you plunge into the problem of supply chain visibility and how to achieve it, we have a few more tips and insights gained from years of working in this area.

Don't forget your people—they should always come first

Systems that offer insights and new ways of understanding the supply chain network don't exist in isolation but need people who can work effectively with the information they get from the system. Focus on your people first by building a change framework and a transformation roadmap that will help you to get the full ROI on the investment into the system. (Refer also to our chapters on digital transformation.)

Have a goal but start with a plan

We discussed the importance of preparation in the previous section but the importance of this can't be overestimated. You know your goal, but you must know the steps to take to get there first. We recommend that you start with a dedicated pilot before diving headfirst into full visibility. Again, as mentioned in the section on supply chain issues above, think about the pain points that need to be addressed first.

Reach out to your suppliers

Once this is established in your own company, you can move to supplier or to N-Tier suppliers. However, as we've seen in our work with a number of clients, some companies also start with suppliers as they see here the greatest opportunities to improve raw material availability and avoid costly production downtimes.

Choosing the right software

Supply chain visibility can be achieved in silos or functions through specific vendors. Visibility truly adds value when seen end-to-end. For this purpose, we see a number of criteria to watch out for when choosing the right software.

- The right uses: The solution needs to support the uses that you're aiming to address. A positive customer experience from the solution provider is the key to a greater return on investment.
- The analytics capability of a solution helps in achieving the efficiency of supply chain processes by highlighting blind spots and inefficiencies. Being proactive and anticipating the future is what will make predictive analysis the next big thing in supply chain business intelligence.
- AI supported: The best visibility solutions also offer AI or machine learning capabilities that can identify patterns in upcoming disruptions— look for real use cases in these areas.
- Security is one of the most vital aspects of a best-in-class supply chain visibility platform. When customer data and business-critical informa-

tion are involved, security should be your priority. Today's cutting-edge IT systems and mobile data collection solutions provide comprehensive visibility by sharing data. All technologies being used by supply chain visibility solution providers also need to share large amounts of data with telematics devices and software.

- Scalability: When searching for a supply chain visibility software vendor, look for vendors who offer technology that is built on the latest framework for scalability. Such technology functions best for cloud applications. In addition, the integration speed with your legacy systems is crucial to your ROI so look for solution providers that offer easy API integration. APIs are the preferred method for connectivity because they make it possible to integrate information from various systems to internal legacy systems.
- The usability of a supply chain visibility platform is a factor that cannot be overlooked. Your staff will be using the platform daily, so providing them with user-friendly technology that has an intuitive and flawless user experience is important. Users should not have to search for the next clicks when trying to accomplish a task.[6]

Chapter 3.5
Call to action: A checklist for practitioners

This chapter presents a summary of the central concepts of section 3 of the book. Challenge the status quo of your company and answer the questions that follow.

Lessons learned: Procurement

WHAT DID WE LEARN FROM *DIGITAL PROCUREMENT: A KEY DRIVER FOR PERFORMANCE IMPROVEMENT?*
In general, both workflows and processes should be standardized to the maximum. Approval workflows, for example, are often a problem for lean digitalization. This is very much linked to changes in leadership culture and mindset, from transactional micromanaging to empowerment and effective management control. Digitalization needs to deliver lean and simplified processes while having the maximum possible transparency and data quality.

DO YOU THINK YOUR PROCUREMENT IS ALREADY DIGITAL?
Evaluate the status quo with the following questions.

The secret recipe for digital procurement practitioners	Yes
i	Are your procurement strategy and your overall digitalization vision aligned? It's not only tool selection and software implementation—it's much more than an exercise in IT. Define your procurement and IT vision first and then rethink the operating model.	
ii	Is your team empowered to understand digitalization transformation and ready to walk along the path together? You are only as good as your team. Digitalization requires a solid team effort. So, bring your team along and walk the transformation path together. And why not try something new and introduce agile working?	
iii	Does your collaboration with suppliers include not only their delivery and performance, but also electronic data exchange, alignment of expectations and open discussions on innovative contributions? Make business partners and suppliers part of the team. Their expectations and contributions are an important part of the transformation.	
iv	Are your job profiles updated in line with the requirements of your future workforce and new ways of working regarding skills, capabilities and degree of independence? Overcome traditional job roles and be creative by designing a team of procurement architects with complementary skills. Less hierarchy, more diversity of skills, and more empowerment.	
v	Do you have the right level of commitment for a sustainable transformation and a way to patiently measure your ongoing success? Transformation takes time and won't happen overnight. In any case, successful transformation requires leadership and vision. Apply agile leadership and trust in your team.	

Lessons learned: Future Supply Chain planning

WHAT DID WE LEARN FROM *FUTURE SUPPLY CHAIN PLANNING: FASTER AND SMARTER?* Planning typically accounts for one third of the administrative roles in supply chain management including the different functions like demand, inventory, supply, production, transport planning and order management.

Planning is already an important role in most companies, but it will gain even higher importance in the future due to increased volatility and rising customer expectations.

DO YOU THINK YOUR SUPPLY CHAIN PLANNING IS ALREADY DIGITAL?
Evaluate the status quo with the following questions.

The secret recipe for (future) digital supply chain planning practitioners	Yes
i	Do you have access to internal and external data sources to maximize the accuracy of your demand predictions (awareness)? The ability to identify and use the right data sources to maximize predictions will be a winning factor in the future to address rising customer expectations.	
ii	Are you ready to improve time-to-action and achieve concurrency in planning with seamless time horizons (speed and execution)? Due to increasing customer expectations and volatile markets, guaranteeing faster order-to-delivery times than your competitors will be a decisive competitive advantage.	
iii	Are decisions based on scenario-based proposals generated by digital tools or advanced planning systems (decision making)? The traditional planning approach is based on a preparation phase to arrive at decision proposals that are prepared and evaluated by experts. Thinking in scenarios becomes a feasible option when supported by advanced tools with learning algorithms that can quickly produce alternatives.	
iv	Have you thought about the future roles required in supply chain planning to take advantage of data, analytics and the power of advanced planning tools (people and mindset)? There will be changes to traditional roles such as demand and supply planners and there will be fewer of them. Prepare for the coming changes and think about the skills and capabilities needed to be at the forefront.	

Lessons learned: Logistics today and tomorrow

WHAT DID WE LEARN FROM *LOGISTICS TODAY AND TOMORROW*?
The logistics sector has become much more important and has grown strongly. As an operational discipline, logistics has become an important competitive differentiator. In recent years, issues such as optimization and digitalization have gained importance in the sector. As in any other business area, IT will continue to play a primary role in logistics.

DO YOU THINK YOUR LOGISTICS OPERATIONS ARE ALREADY DIGITAL?

	The secret recipe for (future) digital *logistics* practitioners	Yes
i	**Have you taken steps to ensure the optimal integration of the new organization and its updated processes?** Close integration between (new) organizations and (new) processes is a prerequisite. For sustainable success, you must ensure that the new corporate structure is stable and well thought-out. The newly defined processes should correspond to the latest standards and be compatible with the new organization.	
ii	**Does your organization have all the data on the relevant material and information flows?** High availability, quality and integrity of data is of primary importance to the success of digitalizing logistics. Management and employees need to be aware of this and act accordingly.	
iii	**Are all parties involved in logistics processes seamlessly connected?** There must be constant, uninterrupted connections between all parties that are involved in logistics processes. Interfaces must ensure error-free data exchange at all times.	
iv	**Does everyone have the same information at the same time?** The success of logistics depends more than ever on how well processes are digitalized, how closely they are networked and how smoothly organizational units work together. Therefore, all parties involved must have the same level of information at all times. There must be no information gaps or contradictory information in the logistics chain. Mapping the entire enterprise-wide business processes in fully integrated IT workflows remains a challenge.	

v	**Are you considering the use of blockchain technology?** Blockchain is expected to improve things such as the exchange of freight documents for cross-border transportation. The origin and transport sequence of every shipment can be tracked and traced via publicly distributed ledgers. These ledgers provide information to all actors in a transport sequence and help to establish transparency.	
vi	**Do you use automatic storage systems, picking robots, autonomous transport vehicles (AGV) and similar systems?** The role of people in logistics is far from obsolete but is changing. People are now needed to perform control functions and to intervene when necessary so this is leading to changes in the qualifications needed by logistics personnel. These qualifications will be significantly higher than is usual for conventional transport processes.	
vii	**Do you use algorithms and Artificial Intelligence to evaluate your requirements, stocks and consumption?** Powerful algorithms and Artificial Intelligence make it possible to optimally coordinate requirements, stocks and consumption. The system continuously optimizes itself. Human intervention is thus reduced to a minimum and errors can be avoided.	
viii	**Do you use the potential that geofencing offers your logistics?** Geofencing is an innovative technology that evaluates telematics and satellite positioning data. Geofencing enables remote monitoring of geographical areas surrounded by a virtual fence (geofence) and automatically detects when mobile objects enter or leave these areas.	
ix	**Have you developed new business models such as value-added services as part of your logistics operations?** Value-added services associated with this can include, for example, the targeted evaluation of data and the provision of recommendations for action planning, the efficient use of resources, the bundling of transports, the networking of logistics chains or the improvement of logistics performance indicators for the respective customers.	

Lessons learned: Supply Chain visibility

WHAT DID WE LEARN FROM *SC VISIBILITY—CONNECTING THE DOTS*?

If you have a better understanding of supply chain flows through the network, you'll get greater visibility, and in turn this information can be used to give alerts when there are issues in the network. Supply chain visibility creates value through the transparency of flows and information along the supply chain.

DO YOU THINK YOU HAVE ALREADY ACHIEVED FULL SUPPLY CHAIN VISIBILITY?

Evaluate the status quo with the following questions.

	The secret recipe for (future) digital supply chain visibility practitioners	Yes
i	**Have you identified pain points, and where processes can be improved via more visibility?** Before increasing visibility, you must evaluate the steps in the supply chain where it can add the greatest value. Therefore, internal and external steps should be analyzed within the end-to-end processes.	
ii	**Have you built a sustainable base to improve visibility?** A common framework for data in your network is the key for exchange, planning and improvement. On this basis you and your partners can work together on forecasts and the coordination of sales.	
iii	**Have you chosen the right software for your company?** Supply chain visibility can be achieved in silos. But it only truly adds value when seen end-to-end. For this purpose, there are a number of criteria to think about when choosing the right software. Check for: the right uses, analytics capability, AI, security, scalability and usability.	
iv	**Is there an ongoing process for improvement?** It is essential that you implement a trusted and continuously improving process together with your partners. Improvement loops should be used and the ultimate target should be a high degree of visibility in the network.	

| v | **Have you empowered your people to understand, work and run tools to increase visibility?** Systems that offer insights and new ways of understanding the supply chain network don't exist in isolation but need people who can work effectively with the information they get from the system. | |

PART 4

DIGITAL SUPPLY CHAINS IN ACTION

Chapter 4.1
Being a leader in a Digital Supply Chain
Kai-Uwe Gundermann, Thomas Mrozek

Introduction

Predictions about the future of supply chains sometimes sound like they have come from a science fiction movie. There are robots, drones and AI-driven intelligence that supports production yet leads to fewer human workers. A balletic dance of robot arms will contribute to finishing products in production lines. Drone swarms will be delivering products to customers who will experience ever-improving customized services as a result of the data they provide.

Through advanced AI algorithms and underlying data, robots can independently automate processes, evaluate strategies, monitor offers and fulfillment. Factories will work as autonomous self-controlled entities. The delivery of parcels is handled by driverless cars, trucks and drones, which greatly simplifies the process. Autonomous vehicles will collaborate with each other and conduct actions jointly. Problems are solved before they occur through the use of predictive analysis machines that use sensors to obtain real-time data from which information can be obtained.

But this is reality, not science fiction, and there are clear precedents for the such revolutionary changes to the status quo brought by technology. When ATMs were introduced in the 1970s it was initially thought that this would result in banks shedding human resources, otherwise known as bank tellers. However, an analysis of the statistics from 1970–2010 reveals that there was no direct correlation between jobs lost in banking through the introduction of the ATM. On the contrary, since ATMs were introduced the number of banking-related jobs has increased slightly over time.[1]

The reason for this is that the efficiency improvements brought by ATMs allowed banks to focus on expansion and open more branches and serve a higher number of customers from cities to rural areas. ATMs also created new positions in banks, with different career paths and different types of jobs.

There are other types of disruptions that also illustrate how jobs changed, like the introduction of the conveyor belt in the production of automobiles by Henry Ford in 1913, or how refrigerators and freezers changed the cooling and ice delivery industry in the first half of the 19th century.

Not all scenarios that we hear today will become reality, but we need to be prepared for some inevitable changes that will re-shape our organizations and the way we work. The degree of shift in the supply chain is not yet fully clear, but there will be a change. Even today, the effects of technologies like analytics and AI cannot be ignored.

There will be changes that will occur and challenges that humans will have to deal with. Supply chain leaders need to be prepared for changing job roles as a result of automation, AI and other technologies that will impact supply chains. Since these changes will also bring significant improvements in the coming years, the speed of decisions that need to be taken will increase. Waiting for answers is no longer an option. Technology will help us to understand, evaluate and solve problems.

In essence we need to be prepared to build capabilities, describe new roles and try to apply new technologies.

Activities today vs. tomorrow

The previous chapter outlined how supply chains will be impacted and changed by technologies and digitalization. The way they work today will not be the way we work tomorrow. In the following sections we will review a number of examples of changes that will happen. We will evaluate the three key segments of today's and tomorrow's work: desicion-making process, case preparation and cooperation along the supply chain.

	Today	Future
Process	• With a time delay • Reactive	• Predict to prevent • Scenario based • Concurrency driven (now)
Decision preparation	• Local sub-system • Specific data collection and combination • Manual and IT supported scenario simulation	• Addressing the value chain and eco system • Analytics/machine learning based data crawling • AI supported scenario proposals
Alignment	• High effort to align and inform • High number of involved staff • Effort to document and communicate	• Decision on the sport based on scenario propos. • Supported by digital eco system • Communicated into the supply chain network linking backbone system to mobile devices

Figure 35: Three key segments of today's and tomorrow's work

Today, organizations often are set up to manage resources, prepare information and execute tasks to improve business outcomes. People deal with administrative tasks that must be conducted but do not add value to the core processes or core value of the business. Employees have to deal with clients and suppliers in order to correctly manage information and material flows or observe errors in automatic data interchange. The workforce needs to have specific skills to prepare documentation and information. Hence, it requires specific functional knowledge in dealing with specific tasks, and troubleshooting skills to focus on function-specific issues or problems. Missing information and a lack of data emphasizes this and requires expertise and risk evaluation skills to define solutions.

We are already seeing changes in the way we work today.

Empowered employees question what they have to do and overall strategic directives. Data needs to be carefully managed as it is what decisions are based on. Enterprises are learning how to deal with data sources using new technologies and smarter algorithms so that these can be used as strategic, advantage-giving resources.

Artificial Intelligence is being used to help make decisions based on scenarios, a self-learning process that improves over time.

On a more personal level, our daily lives are becoming unthinkable without our mobile devices. They are increasingly used in business for email and communication as well as for real-time data exchange to make evaluated decisions anywhere and anytime.

These are only a few examples of how things are already changing in supply chain organizations. Clearly there are traditional supply chain issues that need to be addressed, from missing parts in production to reduction of lead times and improved service levels. Nevertheless, supply chain organizations need to get ready for the changes that will affect their staff.

Automation and other technologies impacting supply chain organizations will also lead to changes in organizational hierarchies, with leaner structures, more peers on equal levels, and different roles reporting to the chief supply chain officer. Very few managers will coordinate day-to-day activities, since those tasks will be largely automated. Instead, they will increase their focus on further optimizing the supply chain network, improving communication and exchanging supply chain scenarios beyond the walls of the company they work for. This in fact means leadership roles need to be adjusted towards managing an ecosystem of people, technologies and resources. Teams will increasingly focus on creating more ways to extract competitive advantages from the supply chain. Managers will focus on organizing and forming the future instead of reacting to current events. Management styles will have to be more agile. Teams will get together more regularly in short meetings to discuss future opportunities and scenarios to solve upcoming problems.

Why is it this important to understand this? Leaders need to get a grip on the disruptive trends in supply chains and the technologies supporting processes along value chains. They need to recognize upcoming trends and which of them have an impact on their business, including processes, roles and the organization they manage.

Leading in digital times

Leading in digital times means that leaders have to be able to cope with an ever-changing environment where everything happens at a greater speed than before. There are people who argue that with digital technologies the future will be more like the past but according to renowned philosopher George Santayana, "Those who cannot remember the past are condemned to repeat it." Then there are those who claim, in the words of US author James Baldwin, "No one can possibly know what is about to happen: It is happening, each time, for the first time, for the only time."

So how do you prepare leaders for this?

Either way, as leaders enter turbulent times in a fast-paced and capricious environment, they need to be prepared to lead their operations with a calm hand. They need to translate uncertainty into a positive outcome for themselves and their organizations by aligning to this new normal. They need to build an ensemble of people and teams that are aligned to the new developments and support the supply chain and other teams with their insights. Relying on one person to know everything is the old normal. Leaders need to promote digital openness and maturity since this will attract talent and develop their own resources into digital advocates to drive innovation across functions and along the supply chain.

Let's look at key ingredients for leaders to master the seas of change in a digitally disruptive world:

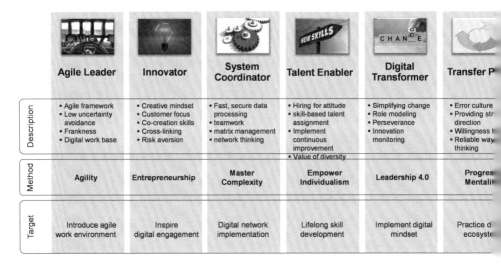

	Agile Leader	Innovator	System Coordinator	Talent Enabler	Digital Transformer	Transfer P
Description	• Agile framework • Low uncertainty avoidance • Frankness • Digital work base	• Creative mindset • Customer focus • Co-creation skills • Cross-linking • Risk aversion	• Fast, secure data processing • teamwork • matrix management • network thinking	• Hiring for attitude • skill-based talent assignment • Implement continuous improvement • Value of diversity	• Simplifying change • Role modeling • Perseverance • Innovation monitoring	• Error culture • Providing str • Willingness t • Reliable way thinking
Method	Agility	Entrepreneurship	Master Complexity	Empower Individualism	Leadership 4.0	Progres Mentali
Target	Introduce agile work environment	Inspire digital engagement	Digital network implementation	Lifelong skill development	Implement digital mindset	Practice d ecosyste

Figure 36: Main changes in leadership tasks and attitudes[2]

1. The Agile Leader

An agile organization is one that will be able to proactively anticipate changes and be flexible in order to quickly respond. Agile teams and companies are customer- and value-oriented. They work in network structures instead of linear and hierarchical silos. Agile organizations are comfortable with uncertainty. The manager is a service provider for the team and ensures that it can work smoothly in any kind of setup in the office or virtually. The principles of this type of agility are consistently high transparency, an attitude of trust, self-organizing teams with effective feedback mechanisms, and motivation through meaningful work.

A typical feature of agile processes is to produce outcomes or prototypes that can be used relatively early. The outcome is a minimum viable product that delivers added value to the customer or the supply chain. This is achieved through the process of repeated improvements and refinements. Agile processes consist of a series of circles involving development and feedback that form an upward spiral of iterative, incremental processes. The proximity to CIP, the continuous improvement process, is no coincidence.

IMPACT FOR SUPPLY CHAIN LEADERS: Make sure your teams are able to work agilely and allow failures along the way, since it is better to fail fast than late. In addition, leaders need to be prepared to delegate authorities, functional leadership to product owners, process leadership to teams, and team development to scrum masters.

2. The Innovator

When you ask entrepreneurs about the way they work, they sometimes look puzzled. Most digital disrupters do not see themselves as innovators. Traditionally, the entrepreneur is an owner of a company who bears the greatest responsibility and the most risks. In today's context, however, the term entrepreneur goes far beyond the actual function.

An innovator or entrepreneur is usually goal-oriented, committed, and does not shy away from uncertainty or risks. Striving for improvement is also a core characteristic of an entrepreneur—even in the event of setbacks and defeats.

Digital technologies have fundamentally changed the way we innovate and how we are able to experiment and test. The goal remains the same: solving customer problems. In this sense it is good to try out and test ideas, especially when failure is viewed as a way to learn from mistakes. In the words of one manager, "It is no problem to fail at something, but it is a problem if we miss innovations because we were afraid to fail." It has also been said that a true entrepreneur is the one that stands up each time he falls down.

IMPACT FOR SUPPLY CHAIN LEADERS: A supply chain innovator is by nature a creative thinker, co-creator, is customer centric, a risk taker, a character who inspires others, and someone who has a keen sense for innovation. They are not only innovators but also intrapreneurs, an entrepreneur working in a corporation or company.

3. The System Coordinator

One of the characteristics of effective digital leaders is their intuitive understanding that the journey is not one to be undertaken alone. Digital leaders need to coordinate the system to effectively bring different resources together to achieve digital mastery. Some organizations address this by establishing the role of the chief digital officer (CDO) and we have seen successful cases where CDOs have been given the power to drive change and manage resources. However, there are also cases where the CDO has failed to deliver the expected outcomes, and where the CDO tries to identify innovation and manages IT projects according to a timeline but fails to manage the people-side of the transformation due to a lack of authority or mandate.

New structures are required to help supply chain professionals and teams respond more quickly to digital change. We see cases where companies partner with accelerators that help bring new ideas, or collaborate with venture funds to access start-ups that drive disruption.

Another option is to hire a digital team. This team can enhance the company's internal capabilities to create a "start-up" that could seriously challenge the company's current business model.

In addition, the system coordinator is the one that questions current business models and drives change, not because of historic rules, but because it makes sense.

IMPACT FOR SUPPLY CHAIN LEADERS: Supply chain leaders are by nature networkers of ecosystems within their organization and outside. Digital innovations need to be accessed through internal and external ecosystems in order to be aware of what is going on and to be a true leader in the digital world. They see the need to question current supply chain or business models to drive innovation beyond their own supply chains.

4. The Talent Enabler

Who doesn't want to have the best digital talent in a supply chain team? This can be done by hiring external talent, which certainly is the right approach. This means you know where to look for talent and how to attract and keep them in your organization. This can get tricky since many companies are looking for the same digital talent in the same places. In this case, there has to be another option to finding talent. Looking internally, and establishing something like a digital talent program where training is given to employees who are bright and ready and willing to develop deep digital know-how.

However, talent scouting is also about identifying the right skills required and having a SCRUM mindset to drive new ways of working, or using analytics to improve the use of organizational data. Digital skills are manifold and cover industry 4.0 technologies, specific use cases as well as digital business models to improve sales and distribution channels.

IMPACT FOR SUPPLY CHAIN LEADERS: Supply chain professionals need to be open to skills that develop and identify benefits for their organizations. It's not about finding what's missing, since new skill requirements will develop all the time. It's about identifying people who can fulfill those tasks either through internal or external training programs or by hiring external staff. Either way, continuous life-long learning is key.

"It will become increasingly important for people to retrain and learn new skills. [...] They'll need strong IT and analytical skills because they'll have to be comfortable analyzing and using data. Then last but certainly not least are social competences. [...] Even though we're talking about digitalization, we'll continue to need people who have strong interpersonal skills, people who are good communicators, and people who are able to work in an international environment."

Alexander Gisdakis, Former Head of HR Leadership Culture, Siemens AG

5. The Digital Transformer

Digital transformation will be covered in detail in the chapters that follow. A key factor that we have learned from experience, and through a recent industry survey about digital transformation in supply chain management, is that the transformation is not technology-led but people-led. A successful transformation involves changing culture, people, attitudes and norms that are embraced by organizations. To be a digital transformer, sensing change is not enough. They need to feel and digest changes driven by technologies and start-ups to understand the impact on their business and supply chain ecosystems. They need to estimate when this will have an impact. If business leaders are not able to understand and interpret these signals, they do not have an advantage over those who did not see change coming. Supply chain leaders need to be the facilitator of change along the value chain. They can be supported by digital transformation agents or a digital transformation office to achieve this goal. But what is essential is that leaders are role models that show perseverance.[3]

IMPACT FOR SUPPLY CHAIN LEADERS: Being a digital transformer requires openness to change. You should use different sources to identify and evaluate changes in your supply chain for your business, such as start-up crunches, conferences and digital labs focusing on supply chain. You should work with partners, suppliers and customers to implement changes into your organization.

6. The Vision Architect

Managers need to interpret what digital changes will mean to their business. The key question is: What are the key drivers and in which way will they become relevant for the supply chain? The vision architect knows how to move from idea to execution in order to translate a vision to reality. Achieving this requires a certain degree of self-reflection, openness, but also a credible mindset for visions to be followed.

IMPACT FOR SUPPLY CHAIN LEADERS: A supply chain leader not only needs to manage the supply chain but is also required to build for the future; the vision architect should plant the seeds of ideas in the organization that grow into a future where networks of supply chains are interconnected in real time.

Typical future leadership skills

Times have changed, so leadership skills that worked in the past may need to be revamped for the future. New technologies have created a business environment with shorter reaction times and highly accurate results. To cope with these changes, leaders need skills that allow them to make fast yet robust decisions backed up with large amounts of information or data.

Another change is that consumers are aware of comparable market conditions, therefore demand divergent and alternative sources. As a business leader, you ignore this at your peril. These new challenges have to be skillfully managed.

The graphic below illustrates four key areas that leaders must strengthen in order to remain relevant, along with a list of facts, traits and recommendations that are relevant to the future leader.

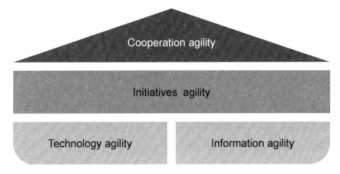

Figure 37: Four key areas for managers to remain relevant

Four key areas managers must strengthen to remain relevant:

1. Technology agility:
   - Technology cannot be avoided, nor should it be
   - Understand the possibilities offered by technology
   - The workforce has to seek every possibility to learn and attend training about relevant applications
   - Actively use new trends around social, mobile, apps and others used by consumers
   - Good news: It will no longer be necessary to understand or read computer programs

2. Information agility:
   - Unstructured information can be transformed into structured data and managed by systems
   - Information quality, accuracy and relevance will grow in importance
   - Learning to make full use of information tools is a must
   - Factoring information into decision making will be crucial but will be automated and easy
   - It will be important to judge the relevance of information
   - Future managers are subject to a permanent flow of information and must therefore find the right time to make a decision
3. Initiatives agility:
   - Routines will be automated, leaving time to concentrate on improvements
   - The focus will be on initiatives that lead to innovation and improvements
   - The role of the leader will be to optimally manage teams and have an understanding of who could best perform certain initiatives
4. Cooperation agility:
   - No silo thinking, but horizontal cooperation across different business units
   - Managers will organize temporary coalitions
   - Teams to manage initiatives will be specifically set up
   - Managers have to support their teams to accept tasks and workloads of differing natures. The work of the typical specialist in line management will differ from initiative to initiative.
   - Initiatives will gain increasingly in significance
   - Traditional line function work will be reduced significantly

Changes on SCM functional skills:
There will also be changes to supply chain-specific skills and requirements that we foresee.

- Supply chain managers will need to be able to see the **big picture through realistic** technology developments. New technologies can overcome current obstacles, such as limitation of information or transparency.
- **All agilities above need to be mastered simultaneously in order to generate a real value**

- Supply chain managers will need to **collect and try out proven technological improvements** to understand and apply these to their own reality
- **Control tower management** will be essential to detect issues and then make related decisions
- **A data analytics mentality** will be needed to consider available information and to judge its importance
- **Risk management expertise** and an ability to quickly assess large amounts of structured and unstructured information will have to be combined to aid robust decision making
- **Business process transformation capability** including team, skills, and culture management, will be another essential skill for future supply chain managers

But not only leaders need to adapt, also employees have to adjust competences in the next ten years. Required competences can be split into different areas:

"First, they'll need to have what I would describe as professional competences. They'll need strong IT and analytical skills because they'll have to be comfortable analyzing and using data. Further they will need to have a thorough understanding of the processes used in the place where they work as well as comprehensive knowledge of the organisation itself, including business and regional units. They'll also need to be a specialist in some area, either in a particular domain industry or in a certain material field. The second general area is what I call methodology competences and by this I mean people will have to be good at using a variety of tools to help them with their work.
Then last but certainly not least are social competences. Even though we're talking about digitalization, we'll continue to need people who have strong interpersonal skills, people who are good communicators, and people who are able to work in an international environment."

Alexander Gisdakis, Former Head of HR Leadership Culture, Siemens AG

Role today	Description
Customer service	The objective of customer service is to ensure customer satisfaction. The focus is currently on transactions involving the associated documents/information management.
Demand planner	A demand planner creates an estimate of future product demand based on analytical, marketing, and sales data. Sometimes, inventory planning is included in their responsibilities.
Supply planner	The supply planner optimizes the balance of inventory across the entire network. The target is to achieve customer service levels at an optimal economical setup.
Inventory manager	Inventory managers plan the inventory levels across the business. They manage stock deviations with supply chain partners.
Supply chain analyst	This role focuses on the collection of cross-plant and network-relevant events that impact supply chains.
S&OP lead	The sales and operations planning (S&OP) leader achieves consensus between supply chain participants to set optimal targets for mid-term-horizon.
Transport manager	Transport managers organize and coordinate all in-/outbound transports.
Production planner	The production planner is responsible for planning material flows at optimal resource utilization and order accuracy.
Logistics manager	The manager organizes warehousing and shipping operations.

Role in the future	Description
Commercial troubleshooter	From service to troubleshooting. Standard information will be provided by information systems. They'll be enabled to detect potential issues, prioritize, analyze and solve customer-relevant problems in relation to specific transactions. Excellence becomes commercial impact instead of forecast accuracy or OTIF.
Data scout/ Data scientist	"Precise prediction is the currency of the 21st century" and data is the leading currency for predictions. A data scout is required to identify external and internal data, structured and unstructured. The scout not only needs to identify the data but also relate to its use and test correlations to the business before recommending them for use.
Forecasting library specialist	He/she runs statistical predictions based on the latest statistical engines and developments. He/she is always alert to new developments and compares best methods including, for example, the R-Library (an open source library) that includes ARIMA and other models for forecasting. He works closely with the data scout to manage and improve forecasts based on best-fit correlations with external or internal data sources.
Sales and marketing insight scout	This role comes closest to the demand planner of today. However, the insight scout's focusing is on planning new products, specific marketing events, and promotions. He/she may be leading the consensus meeting in case required.
Scenario exception specialist	He/she will identify disruptions to the supply network and evaluate these. Scenarios will be created with drivers for business decisions and risk. The aim is to evaluate the scenarios and their probabilities.
Inventory analytics specialist	The specialist reviews real-time and predictive inventory levels in correlation with potential future events. He/she must evaluate inventory drivers and their impacts, monitor and adjust stock levels, including safety stock and replenishment points. The specialist has to track the dynamics and adjustments of stock levels.
Scout and troubleshooter	His/her job description encompasses the collection and evaluation of events that impact supply chains. The troubleshooter defines alternative scenarios and prevents critical situations.
Control tower architect	The architect has to set up control towers and train them to take relevant and optimal decisions.
S&OP athlete	He/she detects sales opportunities that optimally fit operations, evaluates operational opportunities for margin optimization, and creates and stimulates options to dynamically adjust the business.
Customer service manager	The customer service manager aims to continuously improve the customer experience and pushes relevant information to customers.
Logistics transport scout	This role will aim to combine all potential combinations to deliver to customers optimal value at the lowest cost for logistics services.
Customization master	This person will focus on manufacturing long runs to produce low unit costs. He/she manages the increased number of SKUs to meet customer requirements. The customization master has to manage real-time changes to the plan at an optimal level for the company.
Customer satisfaction director	Technology in fulfilment functions will enable more options to build a load, set routes and meet customers' requirement. They will manage late-stage custom packaging and new logistics modes like drones.

Table 1: Overview future roles[4]
Specific Supply Chain roles in the future (with corresponding traditional role)

Impact on roles and organization

We see a change where the next generation of supply chain leaders are well educated and trained to use technologies through all of their respective disciplines, whether that's procurement, planning, operations, or logistics and direct reports are not only specialists in their functional fields but are also data specialists.

A shift of roles will happen, from those that are structured along planning or execution steps (domain-focus), for example, to those that are clearly task-focused with capabilities that can be used across all planning domains.

There are a few futuristic roles that could also apply to supply chains:

We can have a look into the future when we watch science fiction on TV. Not all is going to materialize but possibly a few things are? One example is Star Trek: Enterprise.

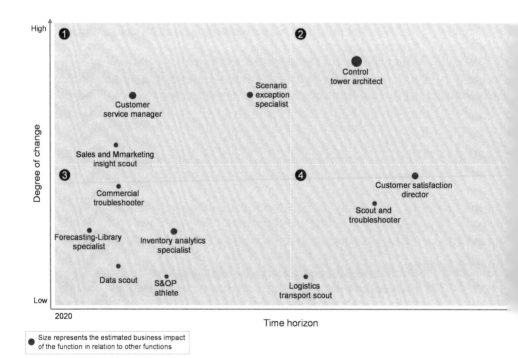

Figure 38: Business impact of different roles over time

Part of the leadership team on board was a robot, called "DATA." He often passed tasks on to subordinates, which they accepted and fulfilled. From time to time, "DATA" even overruled their decisions because of his superior knowledge which was also accepted by his human colleagues.

Leaders

This example shows that the interaction between humans and robots is different from today's life and that the behavior of humans has to change in the future. In order to operate successfully in the environment of AI and robots, the leader must prepare the team and their mindset.

Especially when the assistant role develops into a leadership role, it is important to change behavior and culture. Managers must overcome current barriers and mistrust so that a robot can take on a decision-making role in the real world, too. Alleviating fears will be the key.

Team members

Robots will in certain areas replace humans, get positions in the organization and compete with humans. We have to expect that in the future there will be managers who only manage AIs and APIs with similar responsibilities as a logistics team today.

It sounds fictitious, but it is a reality: Maersk recently introduced a new role to manage RPA and algorithms.

"Recently we introduced a new role, called the 'Virtual Work Force Manager' and it was very difficult to convince everybody that such a role was necessary in the procurement section. But the point is, that he is no longer a team leader or something like that. He is monitoring the robots themselves. He is not coaching a younger buyer, he is coaching the algorithm to improve. This role does not have the responsibility to ensure that the RPA license is valid. The role is purely focused on the business processes—and improving the process and the algorithm. It is not about a new role in IT, it needs to be a business person."

Jacob G. Larsen, Director of Digital Procurement, Maersk Group

As can be seen from the example of Maersk, companies are already preparing for this new way of working. Due to the demands made on people, they become insecure and ask themselves a question: "Am I still needed or will a machine replace me?"

"As a future employee in an increasingly machine-oriented enterprise, they must have a sound knowledge of what the machine is currently analyzing. We'll still need people who have experience of these processes. [...] Employees will still have to know exactly how a certain machine or process works. So for example, a pilot will still need to know how to fly an aircraft even if the aircraft is automated to fly itself."

Alexander Gisdakis, Former Head of HR Leadership Culture, Siemens AG

The fact that this question plays an important role in people's minds and influences them is already visible today. In addition to these doubts, there are three other typical behavioral patterns which can be observed when such a significant change is made:

1. **Cognitive Overload:**
   As a result of the many changes and their speed in their environment. They feel that "everything simply becomes too much."
2. **Black Box**
   There is a lack of understanding of why these changes are made and a lack of involvement in the process itself. Changes take place in a black box. The implementation of the vision and the associated changes are carried out without the knowledge and participation of the employees. This leads to increased distrust and fear of separation.
3. **Force of Inertia**
   It is easier to continue things as they have always been done. To overcome inertia, employees need to understand why changes in their roles lead to better results, are more efficient, and ultimately produce a better result for the organization.

Conclusion: However, the authors believe that the individual will not become superfluous because certain human characteristics cannot be replaced by modern technologies—for example, the ability to solve complex problems or the use of social skills or cognitive abilities to solve customer problems. Modern technologies are most effective when they complement rather than replace people.

Chapter 4.2
Cultural transformation:
The heart and soul of digitalization
Daniel Seitz

Why is cultural transformation so important in the context of digitization?

Lou Gerstner, former CEO of IBM, said that in his experience, the hardest part of a business transformation, including a move to digital, is changing the culture.

What are the key drivers for digital change?

Digital transformation takes time and involves possible adaptations to your business operations, including the talent pool, the organizational structure, products and services, and the operating model (including supply chain processes). Some of these can be altered with hard changes, whereas others, such as culture, need a softer approach.

Culture plays a vital role in the digital transformation of any business because it involves developing a mindset that has adaptability and change at heart. You can have the best, most cutting-edge technology possible, but if your people are resistant to using it, or fail to see how it can lead to a new, beneficial way of working, then it will very quickly become a redundant investment.

"People are the most important success factor in digital projects. It's necessary to motivate, inform and empower employees for digitalization initiatives. 90% of it comes through communication and helping people to understand why we are digitalizing. You have to make the projects appealing and generate enthusiasm by having clear and transparent goals."

Roland Becker, Managing Director, GLX Logistics

Corporate culture can be likened to an iceberg. It's hard to get a complete overview of what exactly it is as roughly 80% of the elements that make it up aren't immediately visible. It's therefore the obvious 20% that can be most readily influenced. These visible elements of corporate culture, illustrated on the top right corner of Figure 39, include characteristics such as behaviors, rituals, and symbols and can be manipulated as part of the process of digital transformation.

However, if a transformation is to be successful, it has to start at the top.

"We start with the leadership team when explaining the benefits of digitalization. It's important to have them on board first before communicating with the rest of the organization. It's important to start with them because without the leadership team on board for a transformation activity, you're destined for failure. [...] There's no quick fix when it comes to transformation."

Jacob G. Larsen, Director of Digital Procurement, Maersk Group

The focus of this chapter is on the role company culture plays in digital transformation. It provides valuable insights into how you can navigate this all-important element of the transformation process.

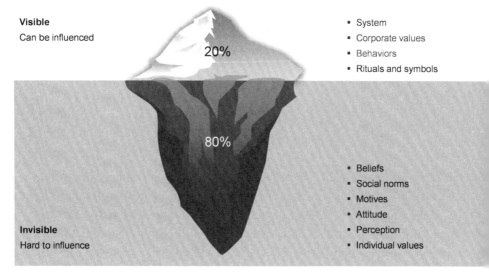

Figure 39: Corporate culture as an iceberg

The path to digital transformation—Some statistical evidence

In our study[1] of digitalization and supply chain management, we found that just 44% of the companies we spoke to have launched a digital strategy or reached the first level on the path to digital transformation maturity. Only 8% have achieved the path to full digital transformation, reaching levels four and five. To put this into context it's vital to understand what we mean by digital transformation maturity and to be clear about how this is measured. An illustration of this can be seen in Figure 40.

This framework involves seven different layers, which you can see on the left side of the graphic. Overall, digital transformation maturity can normally be mapped to one over-riding maturity level. In principal, five distinctive maturity levels can be described and these are shown on the upper part of the illustration, ranging from launch (level 1) to culture transformation (level 5). For each maturity level there are typical time spans from between three to nine months in the launch phase, to 24–48+ months in the institutionalized phase.

Visionary leaders usually drive the digital transformation launch phase but by the time the institutionalized level has been reached it's more likely that the transformation has the full support of the entire leadership team. A good example of this is BMW, where just a handful of people started its Culture Club initiative before it grew to a company-wide movement involving several thousand people.

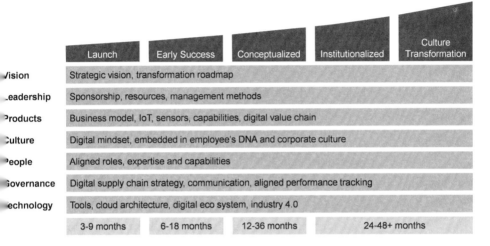

	Launch	Early Success	Conceptualized	Institutionalized	Culture Transformation
Vision	Strategic vision, transformation roadmap				
Leadership	Sponsorship, resources, management methods				
Products	Business model, IoT, sensors, capabilities, digital value chain				
Culture	Digital mindset, embedded in employee's DNA and corporate culture				
People	Aligned roles, expertise and capabilities				
Governance	Digital supply chain strategy, communication, aligned performance tracking				
Technology	Tools, cloud architecture, digital eco system, industry 4.0				
	3-9 months	6-18 months	12-36 months	24-48+ months	

Figure 40: Digital Maturity Framework

In the lower level of transformation, projects addressing business model changes or technological changes are selected because there is a need for change—created by either internal or external pressures—and new technological possibilities that provide fresh opportunities. In contrast, there is a more formalized process for selecting and evaluating projects in companies which are at higher digital levels, very often with a funneling logic and decision gates for predefined levels. In such cases project reporting, for example, has moved from anecdotal to transparent portfolio management. Apart from the expected business benefits, one funneling logic could be how the selected projects contribute to the achievement of the next targeted digital maturity level.

By the fifth level cultural changes are already embedded in the company DNA. Simon Sagmeister, the founder of "The Culture Institute" in Zurich, suggested in an interview with us in preparation for the book, that the cultural transformation needed to reach this fifth level doesn't necessarily have to take a long time and can realistically be managed in a few years. However, it's vital that there's first a company-wide cultural shift before achieving this digital transformation, according to Mr Sagmeister. The findings in our recent study[2] into digital transformation supports Mr Sagmeister's view. The two biggest hurdles for the wider application of digital technologies are the associated costs at 33%, followed by old processes and other reasons at 16%. But at 51% the biggest hurdle by far is corporate culture, encompassing knowledge, people and trust. In other words, if you want to transform the technology and processes used by your company, you'll first have to transform the people who'll use them.

It is important to mention that each function, department and region normally represents a subculture. For instance, effectively managing the supply chain in a global network, where customer demands are increasingly stringent, requires more agility and responsiveness than the work carried out by an accounting department.

 When Satya Nadella became Microsoft CEO in 2014, he began a process of cultural transformation that inspired the company's 124,000 employees to embrace what he calls "learn-it-all" curiosity. As part of this, he replaced the annual meeting with a newly introduced annual hackathon to motivate and empower Microsoft staff all over the world. He also encouraged developers, customers and investors to engage with the company in more open ways.[3] Since Nadella took over, Microsoft's share price tripled. If Nadella was asked how he reinvented Microsoft it's highly likely he'd mention culture change as the driving force over and above cloud computing, refreshing the product portfolio, or acquisitions.

Role of a Chief Digital/Transformation Officer in cultural transformation

Not surprisingly, there is no universal strategy that leads to this transformation, nor is there a standard digital culture focus.

If you want your company to undergo a digital transformation you need a plan and the right people with the skills and knowledge to make it happen. A key player in this is the chief digital officer (CDO) but despite the title, the nature of the role needs to go far beyond expertise in digital technology.

In our 2018/19 study[4] of digital transformation and supply chain management one of the findings highlighted that CDOs have a positive impact on technology implementation and cost control. Despite not being given extra budgets nor free-reign to use them as they would like, CDOs are remarkably adept at dealing with cost hurdles, reducing them on average by 18%. However, they are failing to manage the all-important cultural shifts and people transformation. From those companies that currently have a CDO, the vast majority of respondents (73%) don't feel that the CDO is managing the digital transformation process well enough. There can be a number of reasons for this, including low levels of digital skills among employees and management. There can also be a gap in expectations between what employees think is happening with digitalization and what is actually happening.

In some cases, CDOs might not have the power to align the digital strategy across departments. Furthermore, it emerged that different departments are more or less open than others about digital transformation. This represents another culture-based barrier to the digital agenda and achieving plans for scaling up pilot projects.

Managing cultural and digital transformation? A step-by-step guide

To help clients manage the process of combined cultural and digital transformation we've developed a framework comprised of seven building blocks, as you can see in Figure 41.

Building Block 1: The Why? Strategic Direction and Change Vision

To get started you must first set the overall strategic direction for digitalization in the form of an easily understandable yet convincing change story. The goal for a retail company could be, for example, to become a digital frontrunner for supply chain management, because it is clear that SCM is an area where companies can differentiate

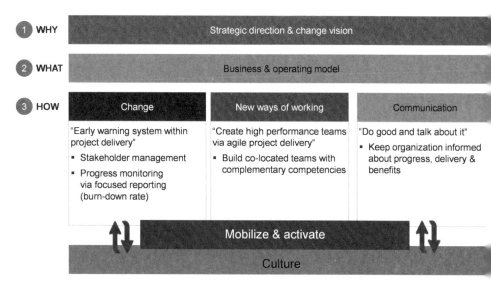

Figure 41: A framework for cultural and digital transformation

themselves from their competitors. Attracting new staff who are skilled SCM managers would therefore be one way of achieving the intended outcomes (the "Why?") of enhancing SCM performance and boosting profitability.

Of course, it's a prerequisite that there should be a defined digital supply chain strategy in place, but according to our recent study, only 23% of respondents have done this.

There are a few questions to ask and answer to help you define a strategy for your company's supply chain.

- Where will we stand from an operational point of view if we don't change (and how about our competitors)?
- Will we lose customers because of inefficient operations? Will our response time be hindered as a result of poor data quality and weak analytics?
- What is our vision for our supply chain? What level of collaboration do we want to have with suppliers and customers?
- What improvements would we see, for example, in cross-functional collaboration, project flows, data transparency, real-time data exchange, and HR and talent management if we do change?

- What steps do we have to take to achieve our overall vision and for supply chain management specifically?

Building Block 2: The What? Business & Operating Model

Here you lay out how the target operating model will be structured. Based on the digital orchestra, a framework for digitalization developed by Michael Wade from IMD Business School (see also Chapter 4.3), the following dimensions or pillars must be defined:

- Go-to-market: What will your company offer and how will you sell and distribute your offer?
- Engagement: How will you engage differently with key stakeholders?
- Operations: How will you modify your company's operations to align with your target-state business models? What's the strategy to support this?
- Organization: How will your organization need to change in terms of its structure and ethos?

The enablers for the operations of an exemplary retail company could be SCM agility, digital ways of working with internal and external customers, and digital capabilities such as using smart data.

"The logistics market will undergo enormous changes within the next ten years. You can already notice it by observing the increase in recent M&A activities.

To be ready for the changes we're currently developing and working on new business models and process optimization possibilities. In particular, we're investigating automation processes in detail because we believe that we can move into new customer segments by doing this and support employees who can do more interesting tasks when simple tasks are taken over by machines.

The question every company has to answer for itself is, 'Are we more likely to be data traders or a pure platform business in the future?' because these will be the two new types of business in the near future."

Erik Wirsing, Vice President Global Innovation, DB Schenker

Building Block 3: The How? Change Story and Vision

It's important to create a sense of urgency to help all those people in your company affected by the change understand why it's necessary. You should create a common view of the digital vision as the "north star," the new direction the company is heading to. Once the why and what have been defined it's crucial to describe an easily understandable roadmap to achieve this—the how.

We recommend conducting management workshops with the optional participation of functional key players. Use these to unveil threats in case of no change by defining corresponding visionary targets and one common message for the entire program.

The "how" could be people empowerment within the digital world and incorporating new technological capabilities such as IoT (therefore being able to connect with customers, integrate with suppliers, execute performance management at sites based on data analysis, flexible response management, and supply chain visibility). Making the best use of reliable, up-to-date data as the basis for holistic analyses and business decisions could also be an important element.

Practitioner examples for digital and cultural transformation

Communication and change management: Stakeholder Management

 To address the concerns of the employees about the changes inherent in digitalization we recommend as a first step to cluster heterogeneous individuals into distinct, homogeneous groups—so-called personas. Normally there are different personas within a company who represent its staff. We often use the persona concept with key functions during workshops to tailor messages to certain key interest groups.

There are some key questions that can help identify the different personas.

- Who are your stakeholders within the company?
- How can your stakeholders be described in terms of working environment, reasons to work for the company, hierarchy, age, or desired career track?

Examples of personas for a digitalization project with a strong focus on SCM can be seen in Figure 42.

In a subsequent step key messages for the personas can be defined comprising vision-based key benefits that address potential concerns. In principle there are two main questions to be answered for each persona when tailoring a persona-based communication strategy.

- What is in it for them?
- What key messages must you develop to transmit these offers?

Implementing new ways of working

New ways of working are the sum of new methods and collaborative ways in which teams work together in order to achieve a joint goal. Current trends such as remote work, home office, and global teams mean that it is vital to consider the pros and cons of new ways of working.

The main objective is to identify change and training needs for project stakeholders and then tailor change and training activities accordingly (avoiding the misguided one-size-fits-all approach). It's important that you not only focus on technocratic enablers such as training and access to tools, but also on motivational factors such as targets, integration in development, and feedback concerning the results you achieve.

To achieve full transparency about the current situation we recommend assessing each stakeholder group to see if they can perform the future tasks and if they're motivated to do so.

The following key questions should be answered to help give shape to a tailored training program:

- What kind of support do the employees need?
- Can they do it (IT, processes, roles)?
- Are they interested in doing it (individual effort, workload, adequate personal benefits—all should be tangible)?
- Do they know how to do it (what competencies are needed)?
- Are they inspired to do it (are the tasks too easy or brainless)?
- Who needs training (h&z online skill assessment)?

	Ralf	Francesca	Albert	Oliver	Victoria	Guido
Name	Ralf	Francesca	Albert	Oliver	Victoria	Guido
Role	Picker in a finished products warehouse	Supply Chain Controller	Logistics Manager	Supply Chain Planner	Head of Outbound Logistics	Head of Supply Chain Management
Description	Blue Collar who fears job loss due to digitalization	Expert who wants digitalization to make life easier	Expert with extensive knowledge, but thinking in silos	Digital native, very skilled, global minded	Middle Manager, trying to protect her kingdom	Senior Manager, not convinced of digitalization yet
What is in it for them	▪ Possibility to explore new work areas ▪ Easy access to information ▪ Personal safety ▪ New ways of working	▪ Less tedious reporting / more value-adding tasks ▪ Personal growth ▪ Understand "full picture"	▪ Gain appreciation for expertise ▪ Possibility to pass on knowledge ▪ Demystification of digital	▪ Work for digital frontrunner ▪ Work from anywhere, anytime ▪ Opportunity to learn ▪ Inspiring people	▪ Helpful for her next career step ▪ Attractiveness for talents ▪ Visibility and control for her team	▪ More time for his team ▪ Business impact ▪ Outside recognition ▪ Attractiveness for business partners
Key message to send	"Your job may be changing, but you have a chance to get ahead of the curve!"	"We understand your daily pains around data. Digitalization will help to get rid of them"	"Your job may be changing, but please help create a digital future based on our past foundation – which you have built."	"Digitalization will help to make a state-of-the-art company in terms of digitization."	"Taking part in digitalization increases her competitiveness within company."	"Digitalization will free up time to spend on more valuable tasks, such as for your people."

Figure 42: Persona concept for communication

Making change and agile readiness transparent

Before a transformation can be started it is of fundamental importance to assess how well the organization is prepared to take on change. Based on this readiness check, areas with shortfalls can be identified and change activities can be developed to address these.

A standardized, tool-based, fully confidential, non-personalized questionnaire approved by your HR department can be used to conduct this readiness. The questionnaire is based on six predefined focus areas (see below) with standardized questions to identify areas of engagement for project teams, top managers, middle managers, and blue-collar workers.

1. Understanding and adhering to the vision
2. Change promotion by management
3. Commitment
4. Culture of action
5. Openness to environment
6. Actions contributing to vision

Introduction of New Ways of Working

It's important to point out that introducing digital solutions for SCM while sticking to traditional ways of working will not work out in the long run. What works well is breaking down big topics into smaller chunks approximately two weeks long and using work packages, or sprints. New ways of working, the co-location of people, and full dedication of resources are prerequisites for successful digital projects. Additionally, reporting should be reduced to a minimum—management needs to trust the results reviews.

There are three main steps to take when introducing new ways of working:

1. Build agile muscles (We understand what agile is).
2. Enable your environment (We have the opportunity to be agile).
3. Gain momentum (We are agile).

Example: Letting young staff and experienced managers benefit from each other

Young and old can learn from each other. For example, senior managers should create awareness about job expectations for future generations while modern ways of working should be introduced by younger workers to experienced leadership teams, who need to be open minded.

We suggest pairing young digital natives with senior managers. Both groups have something to teach the other and there are advantages to be gained from this sort of cooperation. Obviously, the availability of senior leaders who can dedicate time to such a project is crucial. They should be open to learn from motivated yet inexperienced colleagues and should promote compelling outcomes. The so-called concept of reverse mentoring or digital tandems (see Figure 43) has already been used to good effect in numerous companies that have established innovative and learning cultures.

The career prospects of the digital natives will improve as a result of the access they have to senior managers, the visibility they get from working with them, and the first-hand insights they can gain from experienced leaders.

*Senior manager*s will improve their knowledge of emerging trends and learn innovative ways of working. They'll have a chance to re-calibrate—their own leadership style and embrace the satisfaction of passing on knowledge and experience.

This approach generates maximum impact when a few collaboration principles are established before the program gets underway, as outlined below.

- Results are based on teamwork and both parties have to deliver
- There should be frequent face-to-face meetings between the digital natives and senior managers—a minimum of ten meetings is recommended
- Take off your ties and roll up your sleeves—be direct about feedback, speak openly and forget the formalities
- Do good and talk about it—let others know (by blogging about it, for example)
- Let them choose a small task and jointly work on a solution
- Review the outcomes in a management round and reward top performances so that there's greater visibility for lighthouse projects

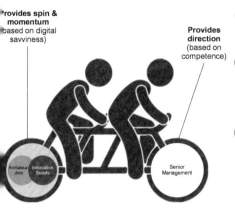

Pairing a digital native with a senior manager
with the goal of **mutual** learning and growth

Provides spin &
momentum
based on digital
savviness)

Provides
direction
(based on
competence)

Ambassa-
dors

Innovation
Scouts

Senior
Management

Benefits

A For Digital Natives
- Career prospect due to access and visibility towards senior management
- First-hand insights from experienced leaders

B For Senior Manager
- Knowledge of emerging trends, new perspectives, and innovative ways of working
- Recalibration of own leadership style
- Satisfaction of passing on knowledge and experience

C For Corporation
- Program as anchor for cultural change (new ways of working, knowledge sharing, etc.)
- Bringing leadership experience & young power together
- Increased employer attractiveness, employee engagement and retention
- Stronger succession pipeline

Figure 43: h&z project example "Digital Tandems"

Capitalizing on the innovative minds of all motivated colleagues

If you want to achieve real, sustainable changes within your organization you're always going to need a guiding coalition of people who strongly support this transformation. Therefore, we suggest you unveil internal, yet untapped sources for innovation by involving employees in shaping the future by means of activities such as call outs, idea runs, and ratings.

The process of capitalizing on the innovative minds in your company is best broken down into four major steps:

1. Frame areas where there are unsolved challenges
2. Reach out to your organization and ask people to contribute their ideas
3. Add details to ideas—pitch ideas—select and implement the best ones
4. Create an execution process designed to implement the most innovative ideas

Communication

Good communication is vital to the success of any project, and digital transformation is no different. It's recommended that you use a communication approach that comprises three main parts: inform, motivate and enable (see Figure 44).

Once you've identified the key target groups or personas, it's important that you choose the right communication methods for each target group—there's no one-size-fits-all approach. Communication is most effective when the messages and methods are tailored to specific target groups, when it's flexible and readily adaptable to change, and managed via modern channels (such as an app). Over the course of our work, we've built up a repository of more than 80 communication interventions that can be used depending on the communication requirements of each defined target group. There are many ways of how you can inform, motivate and enable your people. A few of them are shown below.

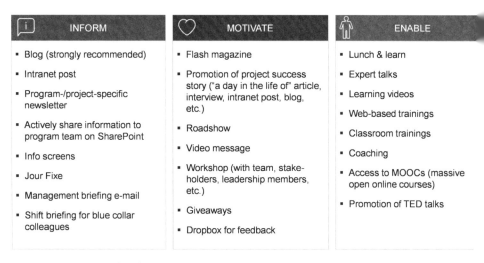

Figure 44: Examples of change and communication interventions

Cultural transformation

According to The Culture Institute's Founder Simon Sagmeister, also stated on his website, culture has come to occupy a more prominent place in today's companies than it used to. It's an issue that has made it all the way to the executive floor and there are at least two reasons for that. First, in a world that's volatile, uncertain, complex, and ambiguous, the classical model of leadership by command and control has less and less chance of succeeding. This makes it all the more important to design a culture that makes the right decisions by itself and is quick to learn and to grow. And second, culture is one of the key criteria in choosing an employer—to many, it's far more important than the pay packet.

There are several different approaches to further develop culture as part of your company's journey along the digital transformation pathway. A very creative method is to select some managers and employees to join a team and then ask them to write and cast the parts for a play about how they see the future culture and operations of the company. They define the building blocks and describe them in a very inspiring and tangible way. The participants reflect on their current culture, what they like or dislike about it, and jointly decide what is culturally important for them.

Another method is to use the Business Culture Design[5] approach developed by Sagmeister. It can be applied in all situations where there is a need to challenge the current cultural status quo and define a clear way forward to a future culture. It shows culture patterns by means of seven value clusters, each represented by a different color and size.

- Aqua represents a compelling vision and open system borders
- Yellow represents joy for progress and learning
- Green represents harmony and consensual decision making
- Orange represents the ambition to win and entrepreneurship
- Blue represents structures and processes and the organization as a "well-oiled" machine
- Red represents speed and determination
- Purple represents tradition and experience

It is a practical way to depict a company culture's key features or changes in the company culture. As a starting point there is an exploration via interviews and online questionnaires. Culture Map workshops are conducted in order to analyze the current culture and define the target culture as well as areas of action to get there. The progress of the cultural transformation can be measured via online culture check and culture monitoring tools.

Cultural transformation: some concluding remarks

Cultural transformation is a prerequisite to digital transformation—it's the mindset of the people in your company over and above all other considerations that will determine the success or failure of your efforts to digitally transform your business. This may seem like a daunting prospect, but a determined, step-by-step approach to the problem makes it eminently manageable.

1. Clarity regarding your digitalization vision and a roadmap about how to achieve it are key.
2. The company should create sense of urgency about why there must be a change and how radical that change should be—this could be in the form of KPIs.
3. The mindset of the company's staff, such as their readiness to try, experiment, and learn from failure is very important.
4. The early involvement of middle management and employees and the creation of user-centric designs will help to achieve high internal acceptance for the new digital solutions.
5. There must be seamless gearshifts between operating models, they must be cross-functional from day one, and silo thinking should become a thing of the past.
6. Ensuring your employees are enabled to adopt new technologies and processes and adapt to new ways of working is vital. Proper training should be planned thoroughly.
7. Proactive communication tailored to the stakeholder groups does not stop in one department or region—all internal stakeholders should be taken into account.

Chapter 4.3
Digital Transformation Office: The engine for success
Daniel Seitz

Introduction

In this chapter we'll look at the role of the digital transformation office and the nature of the person to run it, the chief digital officer.

There are different stages to the digital transformation journey—what we refer to as digital evolution stage 1 to 3—and many different ways of making the progression. As we'll show, there is no prescriptive, fixed way of doing this as numerous factors come into play, not least the size and nature of your business, its current stage of digital evolution and the level of your digital ambitions—a true desire to transform can be a powerful driving force. However, two common factors that contribute to successful digital transformations across different functions and in the supply chain are the creation of a digital transformation office and the right person to steer it, the chief digital officer (CDO). Again, we'll illustrate that there's no formulaic approach to setting up a digital transformation office—there are different types depending on their purpose and we'll look at the pros and cons of each.

Finally, the chapter ends with an examination of the role of the all-important chief digital officer. Surprise, surprise, there's no one-size-fits-all CDO so we guide you through the factors you need to consider finding the right person to fit the role in your company.

From Digital Evolution Stage 1 to Digital Evolution Stage 3— A natural progression

 Broadly speaking, we have noted during the course of our work that there are three distinctive stages in the digital transformation evolution (see Figure 45). In general, large corporates pursue an evolutionary path from the lowest maturity level to the highest (see Chapter 4.2). They follow a logical path beginning from what we've labeled as digital evolution stage 1 to medium and then high evolution or digital evolution stage 3. In each stage the CDO, where there is one, plays a vital role by ensuring that prerequisites such as methods and approaches, resources, technology expertise, and the right organizational setup are in place so that the full benefits of the digital transformation can be achieved.

Some companies choose a different approach depending on their digital ambitions, their internal structures, processes and competencies. For a company with high ambitions but sub-optimal processes and capabilities it might make sense to skip digital evolution stage 1 and move straight to stage 2 so that they can use a structured approach to more rapidly gain momentum.

Although we've seen some evidence to confirm that companies have achieved a structured scaling up from digital evolution stage 1 to the next more advanced stage, Dr Guido Baltes, Professor for Innovation and Strategy at the University of Constance, advocates an evolutionary stage model.

According to Dr Baltes, the different stages can be characterized by the breadth of the digital portfolios already in place. The first stage is defined by one to two projects that are managed in "an explore, learn and improve mode," where the potential of each can be assessed on a case-by-case basis. The second and third stages comprise larger project portfolios and a more structured funneling approach by implementing "artificial markets" with restrained budgets. Here it is advisable to review the projects in a "darwinistic" competition to select the most promising projects in relation to the rest of the project portfolio. Nevertheless, whatever the setup, a dedicated digital transformation office can prove to be highly beneficial, especially when introducing a more rigid funneling process or well-defined structures for successfully supporting the digital transformation.

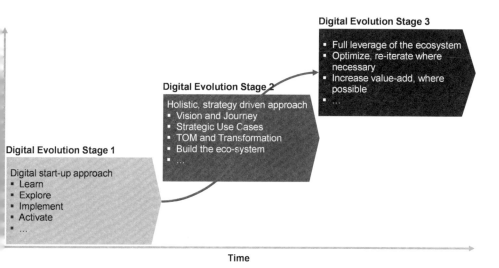

Figure 45: Digital Evolution Model

Digital Evolution Stage 1—Start-up Approach

The start-up approach of digital evolution stage 1 is characterized by its focus on exploring, learning and implementing.

Many companies start their digitalization journeys by exploring digital opportunities from a technology point of view but without a solid structure in place to steer their digital project portfolio. You can compare the digital evolution stage 1 to the start-up phase of a company where a trial-and-error approach is used to test the best solutions, with organizational structures put in place after the business model and product offerings seem to be solid.

This phase has an immediate impact because of the trial-and-error approach, but the overall magnitude is rather small in the long run. We've seen many cases where companies start exactly like this. Often these companies are beginning their digital journeys through idea generation and by building up a digital project portfolio based on their current digital technologies.

This €2bn turnover company established a very comprehensive strategic innovation radar based on internal stakeholders and expert involvement, and by using external technology providers to determine a baseline for setting directions and sharing knowledge. We often see this practice as the starting point of a digital journey. In this case the company even established a thorough prioritization approach. However, we've found from long experience that this portfolio approach has to be combined with a target operating model for digitalization comprising a clear definition of the company's strategy for go-to-market, engagement, operations and organization. Only this holistic view will ensure sustainable digitalization.

However, this company had, at this stage, no defined digital vision. There were no killer use cases defined, nor were there any target operating models and no organizational structures set up to achieve transformation. A further complication was that the mindset needed to get the company ready for a digital transformation was not yet in place.

To tackle these shortfalls, a project was initiated to establish a target operating model that would guide the company through the next steps and improve the long-term impact of its digital innovation activities. A funneling approach was also adopted to come up with a prioritized digital project portfolio.

Digital Evolution Stage 2—Holistic Approach

Once first-stage ideas have been tested in the start-up situation, many companies then face the challenge of transferring this rather unstructured approach into a strategy-driven solution that is characteristic of the digital evolution stage 2 and 3. This is precisely where a digital transformation office could play a vital role. Specifically, the digital transformation office helps to:

- define the vision and journey
- prioritize and describe strategic use cases
- define and implement a target operating model
- build the ecosystem, both internally and externally

This company had around 40 digital initiatives on the go, but all from very much a technology point of view. However, it became clear early on that the company had neither the appropriately skilled people (such as data scientists) nor the resources to fully deploy its digital projects to maximize their business impact. This will normally be ensured through end-to-end coverage of all aspects of implementation such as IT, processes and organization.

The solution was to establish the Digital Center of Excellence (DCoE). This was merged with the IT department to ensure end-to-end coverage of the project lifecycle. It was handed full responsibility for digitalization, from idea generation to full deployment, including IT implementation and, where necessary, possible changes to the company's organization and the processes it used.

The DCoE defined the company's digital vision together with the management team so that there is now a clear strategic umbrella for the whole digitalization journey. In addition, the DCoE has sole responsibility for defining the right approach to the use of data, including what data lake to use, data distribution, and access rights.

Digital Evolution Stage 3

Digital evolution stage 3 is the ultimate goal. At this stage, both internal and external ecosystems are being fully leveraged. We see this kind of setup in separate digital business units like the digital incubator of PALFINGER, called PALFINGER 21st, that have been established if this business unit is fully integrated with the remaining organization of the company. The digital roadmap is fully optimized but, when necessary, it can be tweaked to make improvements. There is a clear vision and targets have been set and understood by all relevant stakeholders. The target operating model is as good as it can be based on the reiterated vision, target setting and the killer use cases that were identified. The different evolution stages will normally be executed topic-by-topic rather than holistically for the whole company. To optimize impact, a constant feedback loop should be installed to start the process from stage 1 to stage 3 again.

The end result of all of this will be increased value-add through digitalization and the use of new technologies, or impact-driven project deployment where possible.

Why do we need Digital Transformation Offices?

 The justification for a digital transformation can be illustrated using a six-layered framework for digitalization. Digital transformation offices, or other units within the company, should organize the all-important six layers to ensure that the impact of transformation is tangible and sustainable. The focus is on the orchestration of all the layers, not on the organizational setup itself.

A good example of this is provided by an engineering industry. After coordinating all layers without a dedicated digital transformation office, the company then created its own digital incubator as a separate unit. This incubator formulated the company's digital vision together with the executive board and related business leaders. It then built relevant strategic radars with potential digital topics or projects to fulfill the vision and avoid possible disruption by incumbent competitors or new market entrants. Top strategic projects were prioritized and given funding by using a very structured funneling process with decision gates.

The incubator is now entering a phase where technological company standards have to be implemented and overarching decisions for technologies or processes have to be made as the basis for successful implementation. It is clearly the intention that this should be organized by a dedicated unit within the company but not by the incubator, where the focus remains explorative and on innovation. This discussion was triggered internally by the incubator to lay the foundation for the successful scaling up of projects.

In order to have a quick assessment of the company's current digital status for example in workshops a pragmatic six-layered framework (in the figure on the left side from top to down) can be used for example as a starting point in the discussion in order to quickly identify the main topics for further investigation. This can be seen as a pragmatic complement to the h&z digital transformation framework (described in another chapter of the book) used in all stages throughout a digitalization journey, but not as a replacement.

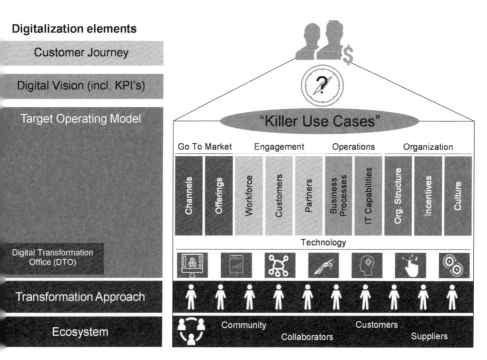

Figure 46: Pragmatic h&z Workshop Framework with TOM orchestra elements

Layer 1: Customer journeys

We expect that in the near future most of the buying process along the supply chain will occur without any human interaction. Where there is interaction, the digital transformation office can help with structural overviews of combinations between customer interactions, channels and products or services. They can also help with touchpoint assessments along the customer journey on the one hand, while on the other hand touchpoints can be compared across other interactions and channels. By doing this, your company can deliver a great experience at all relevant customer touchpoints, something that can be leveraged into a competitive advantage. Here it is worth mentioning that each improved detail in the customer journey or service design can make a difference to the customer experience. Getting the little things right can make a big impact on your customers and produce a wow effect. Imagine how a customer would feel if you proactively notify them exactly when a delivery will arrive or alert them that stock levels are running low at one of their Singapore warehouses.

Layer 2: Digital Vision: Why transform?

According to a 2018 study about chief information officers in the USA, the top three priorities for so-called digital leaders are developing innovative new products, delivering stable IT, and enhancing the customer experience. It could be added that a digital supply chain can enable insights for achieving increased efficiencies, reducing waste and facilitating greater profits. These are clear reasons why switching to a digital way of doing business will help your company. Ideally a digital supply chain comprises processes for real-time monitoring of, for example, inventory levels, customer interactions with products, and logistics providers, which help to increase performance and customer intimacy. It then makes perfect sense to have a digital transformation office to lay the foundations for digitalization and a chief digital officer (CDO) to set the tone and make things happen. According to one study[1], organizations with a dedicated or acting CDO role are more than twice as likely to have a clear and persuasive digital strategy than those without (44% versus 21%).

Layer 3: Killer Use Cases: Focusing on the right levers is key!

Digital transformation brings new opportunities to grow and branch out so it makes sense that companies should embrace innovation, ensure effective customer engagement, bring in fresh ways of thinking, and empower employees to make well-informed decisions as a collective whole. All of this can be facilitated through a dedicated digital office that can bring into play methodological inputs while maintaining a neutral and unbiased point of view.

Technology enablers such as Big Data, analytics, collaboration, and cloud computing are currently very much in the focal point of many organizations. Is this mainly the case because those are currently some of the most prominent technologies in the minds of the executives and practioners? In any case we recommend selecting a few killer use cases with high strategic relevance for your company and aligned to your digital vision in order to focus internal resources, ensure proper management attention, and therefore achieve major and fast impact.

Layer 4: Target Operating Model: What to transform?

Which part of your business should be transformed? This is the fundamental question that you must answer. It's an answer that must be precisely described when referring to the transformation of your value proposition, customers, costs and revenue models, how the company is organized, governance, the new processes needed, changes to IT, and last but by no means least, changing the mindset of your people and adapting the company culture.

The digital orchestra framework developed by Michael Wade, Professor of IMD Business School in Lausanne, and one of our academic network partners, could be used as a starting point. According to Mr Wade, the framework was developed after studying many dozens of transformation journeys. His study concluded that there are distinct elements that need to be orchestrated and aligned for a successful transformation (see Figure 46). This holistic framework now provides a guided and structured definition of all the major dimensions of a successful digital transformation. The emphasis on each particular dimension depends on the maturity level of the company.

The overarching dimensions are:

- Go-to-market: With which service offerings and via which routes-to-market does your company want to approach its clients?
- Engagement: What knowledge and skills does your company need internally in the future and how should you engage with your customers in the future?
- Operations: Does your company need adapted business processes within the supply chain and IT support for the transformation?
- Organization: Does your company need a redefined organizational structure, a new culture to foster transformation, and specific reward structures to motivate management and employees?

Layer 5: Transformation Approach

In our experience of partnering in more than 1,500 projects over the past 25 years, we've seen that almost 70% of change programs fail to achieve their goals largely due to employee resistance and insufficient communication. In other words, this is a leadership issue, or more precisely, a lack of leadership.

Digital transformation requires profound changes and involves more than merely investing in digital technologies. Technology on its own does not drive change—it is culture that leads the adoption of technology. In this case, attracting, developing, and retaining the right talent for the digital age is also a huge consideration—no digital transformation will be successful without the right people in place with the right mindset. Similarly, your employees need to be involved in issues that will affect them if the transformation is to be successful.

Another important consideration is the breaking down of silos so that collaboration is encouraged, and innovation is given more room to flourish.

Clearly there are a number of moving parts that need to be coordinated and directed, a role that should be performed by a dedicated digital office. The digital office could be the unit within your company that works in close cooperation with the leadership team and the HR department so that it can drive the cultural change via a tailor-made communication strategy, a skills development program, and change management interventions designed to enhance the digital mindset within your company.

Layer 6: Digital Ecosystem

In simple words you can describe an ecosystem as a socio-technical system with different participants interacting with each other. The ecosystem framework is inspired by natural, self-organized and sustainable ecosystems. In order to stay competitive and be able to unlock new business opportunities in the future, companies must anticipate what actual and future ecosystems will look like. This is mission-critical because they are currently facing rapid technology advancements which could have the potential to influence or even disrupt existing ecosystems and build up completely different profit pools. We see different kinds of relevant ecosystems during the course of our work including internal and external ecosystems, where the latter comprises outside partners like suppliers, universities, service providers, technology providers and customers.

It can be daunting, but when faced with the rapid pace of technological evolution and digital disruptions in all main areas of the value chain, including the supply chain, there are a few choice pieces of advice we offer to our customers.

- Fully analyze your current ecosystems and the relevant players in them.
- Make sure you completely understand the behavior of your customers and have in place the means to anticipate any changes forced by your customers within your ecosystems.
- Conduct a nightmare competitor analysis: Where can a new market entrant disrupt your business? Often disruption takes place between the company and its clients by establishing a platform at the interface. If not anticipated in a timely manner, the company is reduced to becoming, for example, a hardware or solutions provider while the disruptor is managing the whole ecosystem with the new platform.

A good example of a company that correctly anticipated such a danger to its business model at an early stage was CLAAS. Originally a pure manufacturer of farming equipment, CLAAS has now established a "farming net," a large digital ecosystem managing all different players within that network. But still this wider ecosystem approach has to prove to be a superior solution when compared to its competitors moving in a similar direction.

Observing your current ecosystem and defining a future ecosystem and its role is a crucial step in these disruptive times of digitalization. There are many examples of new entrants, such as Uber, Amazon or Ryanair, that have totally disrupted existing ecosystems because neither the management nor a chief digital officer anticipated those disruptions. Of course, assessing the danger of disruption could also have been triggered by the top management, but experience tells us that in reality top managers lack digital knowledge or have a limited strategic perspective.

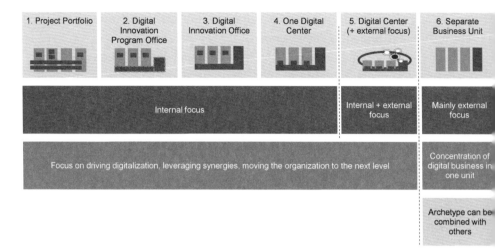

1. Project Portfolio	2. Digital Innovation Program Office	3. Digital Innovation Office	4. One Digital Center	5. Digital Center (+ external focus)	6. Separate Business Unit
Internal focus				Internal + external focus	Mainly external focus
Focus on driving digitalization, leveraging synergies, moving the organization to the next level					Concentration of digital business in one unit
					Archetype can be combined with others

Figure 47: Archetypes of Digital Transformation Offices

A centralized approach, through a dedicated digital transformation office, is the best way to ensure that your company's digitalization efforts pay dividends. There's no one-size-fits-all solution, but from our experience there are six types of digital transformation offices as well as combinations of different types. There are variations that have a strictly internal focus, those that focus on combined internal and external activities, and those that are purely external. The main criteria for distinction of archetypes are shown in Figure 47, and the pros and cons of each type are listed below.

Figure 48 (below) illustrates how the different digital office setups are differentiated based on the five dimensions shown here and represented on the left-hand side of the diagram:

- Availability of dedicated digital resources
- Solid reporting line
- Internal focus
- External focus
- End-to-end accountability

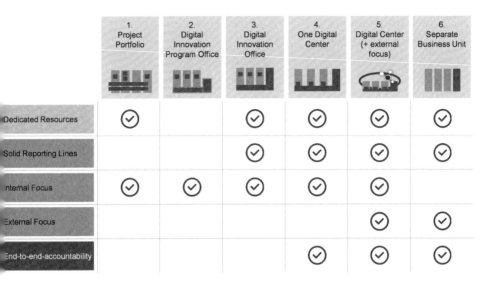

	1. Project Portfolio	2. Digital Innovation Program Office	3. Digital Innovation Office	4. One Digital Center	5. Digital Center (+ external focus)	6. Separate Business Unit
Dedicated Resources	✓		✓	✓	✓	✓
Solid Reporting Lines			✓	✓	✓	✓
Internal Focus	✓	✓	✓	✓	✓	
External Focus					✓	✓
End-to-end-accountability				✓	✓	✓

Figure 48: Differentiating Criteria of Digital Offices

1. **Project Portfolio Approach**
   All company projects (digital and non-digital) are managed and reported in one portfolio. The focus is on functional and cross-functional projects.
2. **Digital Innovation Program Office**
   This involves the coordination of digital activities, such as standardization and sharing best practices, across functions and units within the company.

Case Example: Digital Innovation Office of a large automotive "OEM" headquartered in Germany

The main goals of the OEM's digital office were to stretch the company's digital ambitions by inspiring, challenging, and assisting its various business functions in embracing digitalization along the whole value chain, including its supply chain. There were four areas that were singled out for improvement via digitalization:

- customer value,
- operational efficiency,

- business decisions,
- employee experience.

It did this by establishing a network of digital offices, one in each function, as well as a centralized team who were responsible for the company's overall digital strategy and subsequent transformation.

1. **Digital Innovation Office**

   In this case, cross-functional or cross-divisional digital activities are managed by a digital innovation office. There are key digital resources available. There is a direct reporting line of key digital resources to the chief digital officer.

Case Example: LANXESS

 In a case published by the company itself, LANXESS launched its digitalization initiative in 2017. The chief digital officer heading a dedicated digital team reports directly to the chairman of the board. The main objective of the initiative is to develop and implement new business models and advanced technologies throughout the entire value chain. It is also the clear ambition to digitally enable LANXESS employees and therefore foster the progress of digitalization within the company.

2. **One Digital Center**

   Where there is one digital center, there is full accountability and control of all digitalization projects (functional and cross-functional) and solid reporting lines of all digital resources to one CDO. Although the CDO has an end-to-end focus on all digital activities, the company still only focuses on internal digital projects.

Case Example: Engineering company

 In this example, the digital office was fully integrated into the IT department and given total responsibility for the company's whole digital operating model, including vision setting. It is fully accountable for project deployments, but these are strictly horizontal deployments (within the company).

3. Digital Center + external focus

A digital center with an external focus has full accountability and control of all functional and cross-functional digitalization projects, both inside the company and outside with relevant stakeholders and suppliers. Oversight of all digital resources is given to one CDO who has an end-to-end focus on all digital activities.

Case Example: Digital Center + external focus "Robert Bosch"

In January 2018, Bosch announced the launch of Bosch Connected Industry, an operating unit of the mother company with an initial 500 employees. Its broad remit was to manage industry 4.0 projects internally and those that were directed at customers. Every business sector should transfer responsibility for their digital activities to a Business Chief Digital Officer (BCDO), who will closely collaborate with the corporate IT. By this new operating model, the initiation and launch of digital projects is now coordinated by a global team.

4. Separate Business Unit

A separate business unit can be used to run all digital business and activities. It is characterized by solid reporting lines within the digital business unit and by having all digital activities centralized. The focus is on monetizing new digital business models.

McLaren's Digital Orchestra— New value pools for applied technologies

This example of Formula 1 legend McLaren comes from an article[2] by Michael Wade, in which he discussed digital disruption.

McLaren has a history of performance and innovation. But this did not prevent the company from struggling for survival in the late 1990s and early 2000s. The reasons for this troubled situation have been new regulations and strong competitors. At that time McLaren decided to build up a separate group, McLaren Applied Technologies. The business rationale behind this was to leverage its key expertise and developments for racing also in other industries. One key example for this would be real-time data capturing. The utilization of modeling and simulation technology intended for crash safety strategies McLaren used the analogy of a digital orchestra split into four sections—go-to-market, engagement, operations and organization—to establish a new business model. The unit is McLaren's fastest-growing and most profitable company.

This "digital orchestra" approach is something that we at h&z use to successfully guide some of our clients through the digital transformation process.

The pros and cons of each archetype

Each archetype has different characteristics, as highlighted in Figure 49, and different pros and cons.

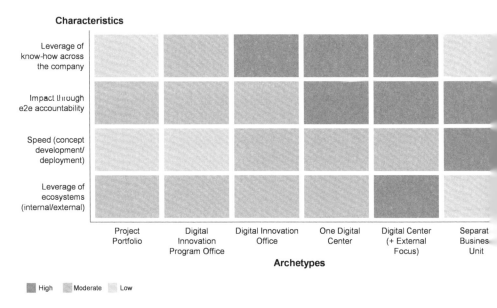

Figure 49: Archetypes of Digital Offices and their main characteristics

With a pure **project portfolio** approach all characteristics are rated low or medium. With this approach, all projects are treated equally within the company's portfolio and there is limited interference in business decisions. It is by far the loosest type of coordination of digital projects.

With the **digital innovation program** different digital activities are co-ordinated. This approach ensures adequate resource allocation and there-fore guarantees know-how is correctly leveraged across the company. Due to its mandate, the different business units usually accept the intervention. On the downside, this approach generally has limited impact and drive due to its limited mandate for deployment which in turn means it has no di-rect influence on value creation through digital project delivery and the de-ployment of digital solutions. A major factor in this is that the head of the digital innovation program office usually has limited power and resources.

With a **digital innovation office**, the solid reporting line for digital re-sources and full accountability for project deployment represent strong co-ordination of the digital portfolio across different functions. In this case, all the main characteristics shown in Figure 49 are medium or high. Decisions and deployments are usually faster due to the clear allocation of responsi-bility and the strong mandate of the digital innovation office, hence there's a lower risk of failure.

The **one digital center** approach with an external focus lends itself to leveraging know-how exchange with internal and external ecosystems as a way of providing new ideas about possible future digital use cases and underlying digital technologies and applications.

A **separate business unit** has only medium leverage of ecosystems be-cause it is very much aligned to the external ecosystem. There is a slight risk that the connections to its adjacent company functions are not as strong as they could be because of this external orientation.

In this setup the use cases are normally selected by the CDO and the dig-ital office and are not owned by the different business functions that they impact—this could lead to a lack of internal acceptance if not managed or mitigated properly.

A separate business unit can ensure speed and agility because it has its own organization and budget. The projects it manages can have sizeable impacts because they focus purely on top-line improvement and growth. The downside is that there might be two operating speeds within the com-pany. There can also be problems integrating learning from the separate digital business unit into the remaining business.

Horizontal digital activities to support business units and functions with digitalization

There are several activities that should be performed horizontally across your company's different business units or functions independently of the applied digital transformation office setup. These are our suggestions:

Horizontal Activity 1: Partner & Customer Journey and Experience

We recommend that you define the products and digital channels to interact with your partners and customers horizontally because normally more business functions across the organization are affected. Overarching coordination between these different functions is beneficial to the design of end-to-end customer journeys compared to an approach rooted in fragmented silo thinking. Segmenting the customer base provides the basis for prioritizing the order in which the digital linking is to take place. We recommend integrating the bigger customers first because they account for a large proportion of the business and they will generate more benefits than smaller customers.

Horizontal Activity 2: Digital Vision & Roadmap

As a first step the company's success factors must be defined before choosing the right strategic direction for digitalization. Those could include for example speed in production and delivery, customized products as well as price and cost leadership. Digitalization can contribute to this vision by optimizing the entire supply chain from procurement to the point of sale for example by the utilization of real-time and smartly interconnected data or data flows. Once you have defined your digital vision and decided which parts of your value chain you would like to digitalize, respective digital roadmaps for functions or business can be derived centrally or de-centrally. We recommend choosing a gradual digitalization roadmap rather than a big bang in order to mitigate risks and manage available resources.

Horizontal Activity 3: Digital Innovation (internal and external idea scouting)

To enable central vision setting, it's recommended that you use a horizontally organized approach to scout for ideas externally. In this way you'll avoid dispersed leveraging of knowledge or experiences. With this approach the external input for strategies that facilitate new technologies can be channeled inside the company and the knowledge can be distributed respectively to the decentralized functions. This can support the different business functions in project deployment and special challenges.

Horizontal Activity 4: Digital Culture and Digital Learning

Use a method of learning that shows how to collaborate digitally and develop personal virtual networks such as Working Out Loud used by Bosch. Bosch has invested over €800m in IT solutions to ensure the "workplace of the future." Working Out Loud supports co-creation setups and has, for example, a start-up incubator in the USA. Bosch invests €250m every year in personnel development via training and apprenticeships to ensure that employees build up their knowledge. Finally, the company collaborates with education centers and universities, and invests in new technologies and AI.

Horizontal Activity 5: Project Deployment

Project deployment for supply chain digitalization projects such as control towers, improved collaboration between the partners of an ecosystem, or predictive maintenance, to name a few examples, can be anchored centrally or de-centrally. However, when it comes to project delivery, it's not so much the organizational anchoring that's important but the decision rights and mandate of the digital office. Can it also make decisions about initiating or cancelling projects? Can it stop projects together with individual business units if targets aren't being met? Is it fully responsible for changes in IT, processes and organization to squeeze as much as possible out of the opportunities presented by digitalization?

Have we reached the peak of the chief digital officer?

According to the 2018 digital office index from BITKOM, Germany's digital association, 67% of companies are up-to-date when it comes to digital offices, but 33% still have some catching up to do[3]. At the same time, there are, according to our own observations, 4,000 chief digital officers operating globally. Medium-sized companies, in particular those that still need to catch up, should look to employ these specialists to gain momentum in their digital journeys.

In the early stages of digital evolution, it can be very beneficial to install a CDO whose role it is to define the strategic direction to achieve this strategic vision. The CDO occupies a central position from where he or she can coordinate all activities within the company and define a portfolio of strategic initiatives together with the other business units within the company. It's also easier to make full use of limited digital capabilities when they are centrally managed.

We've recently seen a high turnover of CDO positions because companies are seeking CDOs with a strategy and technology background who are able to cope with the full spectrum of challenges related to digital transformations. This profile also includes the seamless interaction of the CDO's with C-levels concerning strategic directions and technology aspects of digitalization.

Normally the role of the CDO is only anchored within the organization for a certain period of time. The more the transformation will be managed by the members of the executive team of the core business the bigger the likelihood is that the CDO will consequently disappear.

Are CIOs the better CDOs?

From our perspective, a relatively large proportion of the current CDO's serve the role of a CIO. We clearly see some similarities between CDO and CIO profiles. Both should drive vision setting, should target efficiency improvements, and should observe new technological trends.

As we see it, CIOs are more focused on application development, the improvement of the technical infrastructure, and connecting and scaling up IT. CDOs, on the other hand, should manage those digital projects with a high degree of uncertainty, develop innovative business models, steer digitalization across the board, and improve existing processes via digitalization. They should also drive the establishment of agile working environments and actively leverage networks to start-ups and other external communities that can fuel the digital project portfolio. They should act as a change manager and drive transformation through enabling affected people.

Hints and tips for recruiting the right CDO

DETERMINE WHAT A CDO NEEDS TO ACCOMPLISH: This can be very different depending on your company's digital evolution and overall strategic ambitions. There are a few specific questions that need answers, questions that focus on the major objectives of the digital strategy, growth revenues, creating better customer experiences, the nature of your digital service offerings, operational efficiency increases, cost reductions, and entry into new markets. You must first thoroughly determine the organizational needs and strategic objectives of your company and then choose a CDO with the right profile who can best help to achieve the goals you've set. Our experience tells us that this step could also very much help you to really articulate your targets, and this "profiling" can even be seen as a decisive step in your company's digital journey.

SELECT THE RIGHT ARCHETYPE OF A CDO: Once you've determined the digital objectives for your company it's time to find a CDO who fits the bill. There are plenty of different categorizations or types of chief digital officers to choose from. For example, PWC describes five types of chief digital officer in its Global Chief Digital Officer Study 2019 outlined by Strategy&, from which we've chosen four (innovative disruptor, market advocate, technology evangelist, digital generalist). We've added to this list the digital incubator, who plays a vital role in some companies. Each of these fulfills a more or less specific need, depending largely on your company's current digital DNA, its digital strategy and ambitions. You should mix in the right proportions of the key characteristics of the archetypes to create a picture of the CDO who best suits your company's requirements. We also often see the case that the appropriate profile of CDO will change during a company's digital journey.[4]

The INNOVATIVE DISRUPTOR will challenge the current digital ecosystem by looking at it through the eyes of a "digital nightmare competitor" who is trying to disrupt the company's current digital ecosystem. This ultimately accelerates the whole digitalization process. In addition, the innovative disruptor will provide the inspiration for how to implement digital channels and processes.

The MARKET ADVOCATE focuses on an adapted go-to-market model by digitalization and helps to redefine communication channels and the end-to-end customer journey with clients and external business partners.

The TECHNOLOGY EVANGELIST defines and provides the technological backbone for new digital business models.

The DIGITAL GENERALIST manages all aspects of digital transformation and digital value creation. He can carry out a rapid and comprehensive transformation.

The DIGITAL INCUBATOR assesses new digital technologies, often in a separate unit, which have the potential to fully transform traditional businesses. He creates an environment of exploring and learning and combines innovative thinking and methods with new technological capabilities.

CLEAR ROLE DESCRIPTION: Here again some basic questions must be answered by the management of the company before establishing a CDO.

- What are the entrepreneurial targets for the role?
- What strategic and operational flexibility does it have?
- Does the CDO have veto rights when it comes to business decisions, and is he or she fully empowered to jointly make strategic decisions together with the business departments?
- Is the CDO fully responsible for the deployment of digital projects?
- Does the role have its own budgeting for digitalization?

WELL ORGANIZED ONBOARDING PROCESS: The top management should send clear messages to the company when, or even before, introducing a CDO. This is crucial for internal positioning and how everyone perceives the role. What will be the profile and personal mission? Which CDO archetype or combination will be represented? What will the mandate be? How is the role linked to the rest of the organization?

AN INNOVATION-DRIVEN COMPANY CULTURE: A CDO operates in an agile and uncertain environment and this could spark concern from those employees and managers who think they'll be affected. This could lead to pushbacks or resistance to change and jeopardize the whole transformation. It's necessary to think clearly about your company's culture and decide whether it's already mature enough for a digital officer. The cultural elements of change should be addressed throughout the whole journey. Is the organization ready for a transformation? How will the changes to the company's structures, working habits and ethos happen?

POSITIONING THE CDO WITHIN THE COMPANY: The CDO is not a typical support function. The role influences business and product strategies and future ways of working and therefore impacts the inner core of the company's business model, namely the service offerings, the internal processes, and how to deliver value-add. The top management should give him enough exposure to build up his own standing within the organization. At the same time, it's equally important that top management provides him with the power to act on an equal footing with adjacent functions and business units (for example budget, resources, deployment responsibilities, and decision rights for strategic business topics together with business functions).

CONCLUSION: There is no "one size fits all" solution when it comes to the role of chief digital officer. The structure of the digital office, the profile of a possible chief digital officer and even the operating model in which a digital office operates strongly depend on the company's position in the digital learning curve, its ambition level, and last but not least, its digital maturity.

Chapter 4.4
Getting it done: Proven strategies and a survival guide
Kai-Uwe Gundermann, Daniel Seitz

Typical Project (digital transformation) Lifecycle

As shown in Figure 50, digital transformation typically consists of five main stages plus benefit collection, from idea generation to implementation (and rollout).

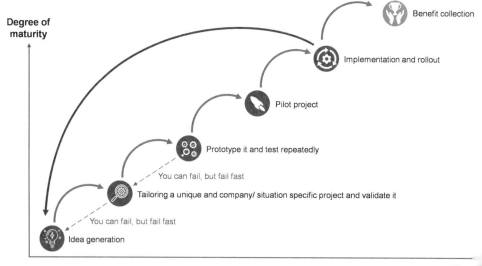

Figure 50: Digital Transformation Project lifecycle. Idea generation based on stimulation

- The starting point of any project is a trigger which gets "activated" by getting confronted with an idea or successful accomplished project.
- The key point is that it is about an external influence which enables the thought that it is possible to realize a significant benefit within the enterprise based on the fact that a forerunner already achieved it or at least developed the main and general idea.

Tailor the idea to a company-specific project and validate it

Taking a general idea and tailoring it into something that is specific is one of the keys to success. This must take into account the particular circumstances and needs of your own organization and in particular its capabilities, capacity, financing, and the timing. There are constraints to every idea and not all of them can be brought to fruition.

Be flexible and be willing to sacrifice elements of the original idea if it makes it more likely to get the backing of key stakeholders.

At this stage it may happen that the project fails before it really got started. There can be several reasons for this such as a failure to get C-level commitment or because the main idea doesn't fit in the company's current situation. However, it is important to keep in mind that failure is acceptable at this stage—but you had better fail fast to minimize wasted time and resources.

Test the idea

Testing typically reveals whether or not the idea has full functionality and the right data setup.

It's crucial at this stage to decide whether the necessary capabilities can be found in-house (taking time into consideration as well) or if a hybrid solution would fit best.

It should be at this point that the main part of the project has been done in terms of applying an idea to a real situation and jointly developing a successful solution with a team.

Remember to go through a test-and-improve phase to ensure there can be a sustainable integration and maximum benefits.

The project may still fail at this point. For example, the prototype might not deliver the results that were anticipated, or other obstacles become too big to overcome within the confines of the available resources. But it is important to keep in mind that failure is okay at this stage—again, you had better fail fast to minimize wasted time and resources.

"Medium-sized companies should discover, develop and implement an appropriate error culture for themselves. In my opinion, a motto for the error culture could be as follows: 'Mistakes may happen, but only once.' [...] To be precise, it needs to be defined how we measure the success or failure of a project, how much time we spend on it and how much we invest. After the predefined time has passed, we have to review the project and compare it to the criteria we set. If there's been no success, we have to stop immediately, even if it's very interesting."

Erik Wirsing, Vice President Global Innovation, DB Schenker

Piloting

A pilot project is the first step towards implementation of a fully functioning program. The pilot phase provides the opportunity to test the idea in a small, defined area. From this, important lessons can be derived, such as resistance to explicit changes within the workforce. In addition, a pilot delivers a proof of concept and validates whether the expected added value can actually be achieved.

There should be a company-wide rollout of a successful pilot to ensure there are mutual benefits across the enterprise. Make sure that the benefits of the project are clearly communicated so everyone understands how it will help. This is vital to get widespread acceptance and usage. It will also pave the way to launch other digital transformation projects.

The successful implementation might become a lighthouse or flagship project within your enterprise and stimulate others to apply your idea to their situation.

Benefit collection

The project should be executed according to the business impacts outlined at the beginning of the initiative.

A process to monitor and measure specific savings should be set up. Establish a system based on the principle of run, measure and adjust so that the project brings maximum benefits.

Many digital projects fail—Some statistical evidence

Experts from the business world have so far disagreed on the question of why a large number of digital transformation programs are failing.

While McKinsey calls 70% of the projects "failed,"[1] Forbes even expects 84%.[2] According to a study by Genpact two thirds of digital transformation projects entered into fail to meet expectations.[3] It is assumed that large companies spend around US$400bn (approx. €358bn) annually on transformation programs which fail to deliver the expected benefits. Despite these findings, companies continue to invest in transformation-related projects. This raises the obvious question of "why."

What are the lessons learned?

What lessons can we learn from digital failures, and how do we increase the chances of success?

LESSON 1: For a successful transformation it is crucial that projects are not limited to a certain period of time and that they can be considered independently of each other. Rather, transformation must be seen as a continuous process in which several projects interact.

LESSON 2: Recognize that digital transformation is not an IT project. Too often, you hear companies implement an IT project and refer to it as "digital transformation." An IT project per se is not a digital project. Digital projects lead to changes in all parts of a company such as people, technology and culture.

LESSON 3: In order to make transformation projects successful, changes are necessary in traditional areas such as research and development, strategy and project management. Leading companies in the field of transformation are aware of this and have already adapted their approaches. Traditional approaches with project delivery in a waterfall manner just don't work anymore. Rather, an agile and customer-oriented process must be developed that meets the requirements of the customer and the employees.

LESSON 4: Most companies focus too much on the technology also when selecting digital projects to build up their project pipeline. During implementation, it is assumed that the technologies (cloud, social, Big Data & analytics or IoT) will behave as in the demo. The fundamental flaw in this assumption is that every company has individual people, data, processes and culture. An example is an incident at the British NHS: A digital service messenger bot accidentally sent 850,000 emails to patients, causing a server failure. They held their consulting partner responsible for the problem. However, who is really responsible?[4]

LESSON 5: "After a digital project delivery is before a digital project delivery." Be aware that digitalization is a continuous process rather than a one-time effort. Plan for life after the program go-live. When is the right time for a launch? What are the reasons for employees to use the new procedure? Which areas of the company are affected, and are they individuals or entire groups? Are there KPIs that I can use to measure the success of the project?

Even if the lessons mentioned above do not provide a solution for every problem in the sense of a standardized "toolbox," they can still be seen as guidelines. Understanding the lessons can make a significant contribution to the success of a project.

What are the strategies to succeed?

Figure 51 summarizes some strategies that have led to successful rollouts of digital projects. The structuring parameters for this framework consist of the different core elements of digital projects shown on the left of the chart and the range of digital maturity stages in the upper row.

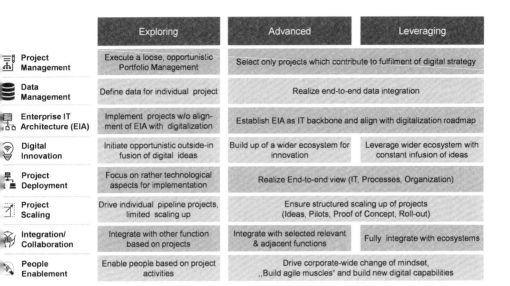

	Exploring	Advanced	Leveraging
Project Management	Execute a loose, opportunistic Portfolio Management	Select only projects which contribute to fulfilment of digital strategy	
Data Management	Define data for individual project	Realize end-to-end data integration	
Enterprise IT Architecture (EIA)	Implement projects w/o alignment of EIA with digitalization	Establish EIA as IT backbone and align with digitalization roadmap	
Digital Innovation	Initiate opportunistic outside-in fusion of digital ideas	Build up of a wider ecosystem for innovation	Leverage wider ecosystem with constant infusion of ideas
Project Deployment	Focus on rather technological aspects for implementation	Realize End-to-end view (IT, Processes, Organization)	
Project Scaling	Drive individual pipeline projects, limited scaling up	Ensure structured scaling up of projects (Ideas, Pilots, Proof of Concept, Roll-out)	
Integration/ Collaboration	Integrate with other function based on projects	Integrate with selected relevant & adjacent functions	Fully integrate with ecosystems
People Enablement	Enable people based on project activities	Drive corporate-wide change of mindset, „Build agile muscles" and build new digital capabilities	

Figure 51: Framework for digital norm strategies

The core elements of the different approaches that are used for digital projects depend on the maturity stage of the company (see Chapter 4.3 for a detailed explanation of digital maturity stages).

Here we focus on the appropriate tactics for organizations at the digital maturity stages "Advanced" and "Leveraging." The reason for this is that companies at the digital maturity stage "Exploring" do not really have a digital strategy or structure in place. Their approach is opportunistic and driven by unstructured ideas from outside concerning digital possibilities. Typically, they run a few digital projects and manage them like other IT projects using a looser, project management and portfolio approach.

The "Advanced" digital stage is characterized by a more structured approach towards digital projects. A typical company at this stage of digital maturity has started building a digital project pipeline and is evaluating projects case-by-case on the basis of their financial impacts. In addition, companies at this stage are in the process of creating a wider digital ecosystem with external partners.

At the digital stage "Leveraging" a typical company has a very structured approach to digitalization by means of a stage-gated innovation pipeline and a formalized process for evaluating projects. By this stage, they are fully leveraging their digital ecosystem to ensure there is a constant exchange of information and flow of new ideas between themselves and their external partners.

PROJECT MANAGEMENT: At stage "Exploring," digital projects are handled in what could be described as a traditional project portfolio approach where the selection of projects is fairly unstructured. Often new technology is the starting point for project selection. Companies at digital maturity stages "Advanced" or "Leveraging" have clear visions about which targets, or the next evolutionary stage, they would like to reach via digitalization, and the financial impacts they hope to gain. Each digital project will be assessed on whether it contributes to these targets before it is selected.

Project Management—Hints for executives: Ask yourself the following questions to help build up a portfolio of digital projects that are fully aligned to your digital vision:	Yes
Do we have a digital vision which clearly outlines the next envisaged evolutionary stage we would like to reach to achieve digitalization?	
Have we collected, described, evaluated and prioritized the right digital projects which contribute most to achieving our digital vision?	

DATA MANAGEMENT: To get the most out of digitalization projects in companies that are already at the "Advanced" stage or above, it is essential to structure and manage data so that there is end-to-end visibility across all the different functions in the company. Imagine a newly established customer journey for an automotive supplier with 15 different customer touchpoints along the purchasing and delivery lifecycle. Clearly, for this Tier 1 supplier it is a prerequisite that there is an uninterrupted data flow across purchasing, production, quality management and logistics to ensure that the user experience is seamless. Data scientists who can build and structure proper data flow management systems are a scarce commodity, so this is a big impediment for companies with digital ambitions. While there will be a fully functioning IT department within the company, it is highly unlikely that there is a digital transformation office, so integrating data management into the IT department would be a good first step.

Data Management—Hints for executives: You should ask yourself the following questions, the answers to which will help lay the appropriate data foundation for your selected digital projects:	Yes
Do we have a clear understanding of the data requirements for our digital projects?	
Do we have the in-house know-how to structure the data flow across all functions?	
How do we ensure the appropriate split between data management governance, data management execution and data management quality assurance?	

ENTERPRISE APPLICATION INTEGRATION (EAI): Supporting successful digital transformations in companies with a more advanced digital maturity requires a concept that aligns governance, processes and talent models with the requirements of the new organization. It should also promote effective collaboration between business and IT. Too much focus on technology can lead EAI teams to organize their work around application development rather than focus on running the business. Companies setting out on their digital journey normally begin their digital projects without having a clear EAI backbone in place and therefore miss out on the opportunity to fully exploit the potentials of end-to-end digital solutions across the entire value chain.

It makes sense to start with a clear target architecture and allow sufficient time to build the strategy based on the future.

Apart from IT expertise, enterprise architects of the future need a broad array of skills to convince business representatives about IT perspectives, including communication, coaching, problem solving, and end-to-end process understanding.

EAI—Hints for executives: Answer the following questions to ensure you have the right enterprise IT architecture in place for your digital projects:	Yes
Do we have the EAI backbone in place for our digital projects?	
Do we need a comprehensive EAI backbone for our selected digital projects?	
Do we have a holistic approach for enterprise architecture that integrates differing perspectives like IT, governance, processes and competencies?	

DIGITAL PROJECT DEPLOYMENT: As was pointed out in the Lessons Learned section, digital frontrunners will already have an end-to-end view of their digital project deployments. Digital transformation projects are not pure technology projects—they can have a profound effect on related process and organization, specifically the people who work there. To get the utmost value from these projects, therefore, it makes sense to take into account all parts of the business that will be affected, including workflows, data, people and the organization itself. To achieve this, the leaders of the digital project must have a mandate to make decisions that impact everything connected to the project. It is advisable to coordinate project deployment centrally (see Chapter 4.3 on the role of the digital transformation office) to ensure that agile deployment approaches such as scrum, design thinking, and sprints, are compliant with global project standards and targets. By default, digitalization should already be considered in business projects along with the early involvement of digital experts. To help install this digital mindset, it is recommended that companies at the digital maturity stages "Advanced" and "Leveraging" incorporate digitalization in their business targets.

Project deployment—Hints for executives: You should question your approach to deploying digital projects in order to fully exploit their impacts:	Yes
Do we have the right competencies on board to deploy digital projects (e. g. IT, process and organizational know-how)?	
Can we ensure agile project deployment (e. g. scrums, design thinking, sprints)?	
Have we empowered the project managers for digital projects sufficiently? Do they have the mandate to contribute to strategic decisions about whether or not projects are successful or continuing and upscaling projects that have the desired ROIs?	
Do we have a taskforce for agile challenges?	

PROJECT SCALING: Once you have closed any excellence gaps that existed between the units or regions and have a harmonized process landscape, the next step is to scale up successful pilots.

"We also noticed pushbacks in certain areas when people tried, for example, to automate product packaging. We realized that processes have to be harmonized first. The catchword here is standardization. If the technologies are used correctly, they force you to standardize your processes."

Peter Dressler, Senior Director Logistics, Infineon

By doing so you can build up a self-financing project pipeline, where successfully scaled pilots will generate savings to finance other pilots or proof-of-concept projects that are in the pipeline. To do so you should define a clear business case concerning the ROI of each digital project. Once this ROI target has been achieved in the pilot, the next step is to scale up the respective digital solution across the board. But you should also be ready to recognize projects that have not paid off.

Project Scaling—Hints for executives: Answer the following questions to maximize the digital potential within your entire company:	Yes
Do we have clear guidelines for scaling up our digital projects (e.g. proof-of-concept projects, pilot projects)?	
Do we have a clear understanding about the expected impact of our digital projects?	
Do we have dedicated resources for project delivery with appropriate steering and governance?	

INTEGRATION AND COLLABORATION: Digital projects are far more transformative than mere IT ventures. It is therefore mission-critical for success to have an integrative and collaborative approach when designing and implementing digital projects.

There are five areas where integration and collaboration are key to the success of digital transformation projects: data flow, data lakes, business requirements, application management, and operations technology.

Integration and Collaboration—Hints for executives: Answer the following questions to ensure there is seamless integration between information management, operations technology, and data:	Yes
Have we assigned responsibility for end-to-end information management, operations technology, and data?	
How do we ensure we are using digital-by-design of machines in production or logistics (e. g. Center of Excellence)?	
Do we have an integrated view? What is desirable from a business perspective and what is feasible from a digital technology point of view?	

PEOPLE ENABLEMENT: AGILE PROJECT DEPLOYMENT, AGILE WAYS OF WORKING: Continuous, high-speed communications and the latest digital technologies have paved the way for agile working. We strongly believe that digitalization without changing traditional working styles will lead to problems and failure. It is therefore recommended to apply agile project management methods to digital pilot projects and, by doing so, leading by example. These pilots will produce quick results and provide vital information on constraints to the organization, its processes, and its people prior to global project scale-ups or rollouts.

There is a wide spectrum of agile approaches to digital projects. These includes for example scrum which contains clear rules and instruction manuals; methods, processes, and procedures. These can be used to systematically get things done and help in applying the right tools, such as sprints, release planning, or stand-ups. Methodology combining different methods like design thinking or Hoshin Kanri are also part of the agile approaches. Finally, mindsets or attitudes that influence reasoning, such as action before planning, problem/solution space, and the diverge versus converge approach can be applied in digital projects.

People enablement—Some Hints for Executives: Answer the following general questions to understand what it takes to become agile: How agile is the current project management in our company?	Yes
Communication: Is it open, face-to-face?	
Work processes: Are they adaptive? Is there continuous improvement?	

Team organization: Are teams self-organized and interdisciplinary?	
Customer inclusion: Is it constant?	
Requirement changes: Are they easy and do they have the right support?	
Team Planning: Is it continuous, with clear target setting?	
Then there are a number of general questions concerning current team competencies: 1	**Yes**
Do we have a scaled agile framework?	
Do we have a scrum master training in place?	
How agile is our current project management?	

CONCLUSION: We have outlined several well-proven strategies to successfully deliver digital programs. As an executive you should answer the basic questions presented here to reveal whether or not you have chosen the right setup for your digital roadmap. The underlying assumption is that digital projects have to be managed holistically, which means that the different parts such as, for example, technology, project delivery, collaboration, and people enablement, have to be addressed at the same time. We could even call this comprehensive setup a target operating model in order to make clear that delivering digital projects involves much more than focusing solely on the technology aspect of idea generation, testing, piloting, and deployment.

Good news: If you encounter gaps in your digital approach you normally can close them relatively quickly because it is not always necessary to anchor the missing key elements within an established organizational setup—temporary, project-driven solutions are also fine.

Bad news: Unfortunately, we can only confirm the statement from Mr Zehnder, the COO of PALFINGER AG, in his letter at the beginning of this book. It is important that you find your own way through digital transformation. There is no prescriptive path, no one-size-fits-all solution for digitalization because each company situation is different in terms of its current status, organizational setup, digital challenges or digital ambition level. But nevertheless, you can follow some patterns or approaches that have already proved to be successful.

Chapter 4.5
Call to action: A checklist for practitioners

In this chapter you will find a summary of the previous section's central concepts. Challenge the status quo of your company and answer the questions.

Lessons learned: Being a leader in a Digital Supply Chain

WHAT DID WE LEARN ABOUT *LEADING IN TIMES OF DIGITAL SUPPLY CHAINS*?
The future of CSCO will be full of challenges. Supply chain leaders need to be prepared for changing job roles as a result of automation, AI, and other technologies that will impact supply chains. Due to the increasing speed of new developments, decisions need to be taken quicker. Waiting for answers and not reacting to changes is no longer an option.

		Yes
i	**Do you have a clear image of how processes, decisions, and alignments will change in the future of managing supply chains?** Leaders need to get a grip on the disruptive trends in supply chains and the technologies which support the processes along value chains. They need to recognize upcoming trends and which of them have an impact on their business, including processes, roles, and the organization they manage.	
ii	**Are you preparing your leaders to lead in the digital age?** Leaders have to master the key ingredients agility, entrepreneurship, mastering complexity, empowering individualism, and leadership 4.0. They also need to have a progress mentality to cope with the change in a digitally disruptive world. The individual focus depends on the aspired target state of digitalization.	
iii	**Do you have a clear image of the leadership skills required in the future?** Times have changed, so leadership skills that worked in the past may need to be revamped for the future. There are four key areas that leaders must strengthen in order to remain relevant: corporation agility, initiative agility, technology agility, and information agility.	
iv	**Do you understand the impact of digitalization on SCM roles and organization?** The next generation of supply chain leaders are well educated and trained to use technologies through all of their respective disciplines. We will undoubtedly see a shift in roles. Possible changes in roles alongside the supply chain have been outlined in detail in this chapter.	

Lessons learned: Cultural transformation: The heart and soul of digitalization

WHAT DID WE LEARN ABOUT *CULTURAL TRANSFORMATION: THE HEART AND SOUL OF DIGITALIZATION?*

Corporate culture, if not effectively transformed and guided into the new century, can be by far the biggest hurdle for a wider application of digital technologies in an organization. It plays a vital role in the digital transformation process because it involves a mindset change among the employees and especially the management team.

Do you think you have the right corporate culture and your employees are ready for the digital transformation? Evaluate the status quo with the following questions:		Yes
i	Do you have an easily understandable and convincing change story? Corporate culture begins with a clear vison of what kind of organization you want to be. It is important that people are convinced by the transformation and know which advantages they will enjoy if they support the transformation project.	
ii	Is your business and operation model ready for the digital transformation? You need the right tools and processes to enable your employees to successfully implement the digital transformation. Help your employees by defining strategic targets on topics such as markets, future engagement, operations, and your organization as a whole.	
iii	Do you have a clear roadmap on how you will achieve the change vision? Design a transparent communication and change management roadmap to convince all your employees. It is essential to cluster homogenous groups, create a common end goal and adapt the communication to their beliefs and thoughts. Show your employees how their working life will be changing and communicate it in a manner that specifically targets the audience.	

Lessons learned: Digital Transformation Office: The engine for success

WHAT DID WE LEARN ABOUT *DIGITAL TRANSFORMATION OFFICE: THE ENGINE FOR SUCCESS*?

Digital transformation is not achieved in one day. In line with the digital ambition, an organization could choose a suitable type of digital transformation office to guide and structure the desired transformation.

Do you think you can orchestrate all the layers of transformation? Evaluate the status quo with the following questions:	Yes
i Did you choose the right key levers to focus on? Technology enablers such as Big Data, analytics, collaboration, and cloud computing are currently very much in the focal point of many organizations. Select a few killer use cases with high strategic relevance for your company.	
ii Do you have an agile ecosystem management? Digital ecosystems will need constant adjustments. In order to stay competitive and be able to unlock new business opportunities in the future, companies must anticipate what actual and future ecosystems will look like.	
iii Does the setup of your digital transformation office support your digital vision? Digital office setups are differentiated based on five dimensions. There are variations that have a strictly internal focus, those that focus on combined internal and external activities, and those that are purely external.	
iv Have you recruited the right profile for a Digital Transformation Officer? Once you've determined the digital objectives for your company it's time to find a CDO who fits the bill. In order to find the right person, you have to clearly define the entrepreneurial targets and the mandate for this role before starting your recruiting efforts.	

Lessons learned: Getting it done:
Proven strategies and a survival guide

WHAT DID WE LEARN ABOUT *PROVEN STRATEGIES AND A SURVIVAL GUIDE*?
There are well proven strategies and approaches regarding digital projects for certain digital maturity stages of the company.

		Yes
i	**Do you have a clear understanding what the current digital stage of your company is?** The stages "Advanced" and "Leveraging" have a more structured approach towards digital projects. Companies at these stages have started to build up a digital project pipeline ("Advanced") or fully leverage their digital ecosystem ("Leveraging").	
ii	**Did you have the right setup for your digital roadmap?** Companies in digital stage "Advanced" or "Leveraging" have to manage digital projects holistically, with all relevant elements, such as technology, project deployment, people enablement, and collaboration, being addressed at the same time.	
iii	**Have you decided to anchor the possibly missing key elements for your digital approach within an established organizational setup or temporarily?** Existing gaps can be closed very quickly by temporary, project-driven solutions rather than new organizational setups.	
iv	**Have you already defined your own way for your digital roadmap?** There is no prescriptive path, no one-size-fits-all solution for digitalization, because each company situation is different in terms of its current status, organizational setup, digital challenges or digital ambition level.	

Endnotes

General Introduction

1 Roither, H., 2017. PALFINGER organized Austrias largest digitalization. URL https://www.palfinger.com/en/news/palfinger-organized-austrias-largest-digitalization-hackathon_n_4509.

Building blocks of the Digital Supply Chain

1 Bloomberg, J., 2019. Digitization, Digitalization, And Digital Transformation: Confuse Them At Your Peril. Forbes. URL https://www.forbes.com/sites/jasonbloomberg/2018/04/29/digitization-digitalization-and-digital-transformation-confuse-them-at-your-peril/ and Prause, J., 2016. Digitization vs. Digitalization—Wordplay or World View? SAP News Cent. URL https://news.sap.com/2016/05/digitization-vs-digitalization-wordplay-or-world-view/.

2 Luber, S., Litzel, N., 2017. Was ist Digital Transformation? URL https://www.bigdata-insider.de/was-ist-digital-transformation-a-626446/.

3 Decide, 2018. The Present and Future of Advanced Analytics. Decide Soluciones. URL https://decidesoluciones.es/en/present-and-future-advanced-analytics/.

4 Gupta, R., 2018. Multi-Technology: The Future of Geolocation. IoT All. URL https://www.iotforall.com/future-geolocation-multi-technology/.

5 Rosenberg, M., 2018. Blockchain for the Swedish Fund Market. URL https://pdfs.semanticscholar.org/2d83/23c05748c421777c039d839cdfffa4ffd35d.pdf.

6 Goldin, P., 2019. Shaky Consumer Confidence in Self-Driving. URL https://www.itsdigest.com/.

7 Xuan, F.C.Y., 2018. Autonomous Vehicles for Effective Supply Chain. SIPMM Inst. URL https://sipmm.edu.sg/autonomous-vehicles-effective-supply-chain/.

8 EOS, n. d. EOS Industrial 3D printing—Process, method and benefits. URL https://www.eos.info/additive_manufacturing/for_technology_interested.

9 Nkwocha, K., 2018. Mike Mulica: How geolocation and tracking can revolutionise logistics and supply chain management. My Logist. Mag. URL http://mylo gisticsmagazine.com/logistics/freight_forwarder/mike-mulica-geolocation-tra cking-can-revolutionise-logistics-supply-chain-management/.

10 Frick, T. W., 2018. Augmented Reality: Chancen in der Fertigungsindustrie, Projektbeispiele. Ind.-Wegweis. URL https://industrie-wegweiser.de/augmente d-reality/.

11 Gesing, B., Peterson, S. J., Michelsen, D. D., 2018. Artificial Intelligence in Logistics. URL https://www.logistics.dhl/content/dam/dhl/global/core/documen ts/pdf/glo-core-trend-report-artificial-intelligence.pdf.

12 Küpper, D., Lorenz, M., Knizek, C., Kuhlmann, K., Maue, A., Lässig, R., Buchner, T., 2019. Advanced Robotics in the Factory of the Future. https://www.bcg. com. URL https://www.bcg.com/de-de/publications/2019/advanced-robotics-factory-future.aspx.

Advanced Analytics—Powerful and indispensable

1 Reinsel, Gantz and Ryding, 2018. "The Digitization of the World: From Edge to Core." URL https://www.seagate.com/files/www-content/our-story/trends/files/ idc-seagate-dataage-whitepaper.pdf.

2 Wang, G., Gunasekaran, A., Ngai, E. W. T., Papadopoulos, T., 2016. Big data analytics in logistics and supply chain management: Certain investigations for research and applications. Int. J. Prod. Econ. 176, 98–110.

3 Nguyen, T., Zhou, L., Spiegler, V., Leromon, P., Lin, Y., 2017. Big data analytics in supply chain management: A state-of-the-art literature review. https://www. academia.edu/37169247/Big_data_analytics_in_supply_chain_management_ A_state-of-the-art_literature_review and Assuncao, M. D., Calheiros, R. N., Bianchi, S., Netto, M. A. S., Buyya, R., 2015. Big Data Computing and Clouds: Trends and Future Directions. J. Parallel Distrib. Comput. 79–80, 3–15. https:// doi.org/10.1016/j.jpdc.2014.08.003.

4 Kumar and Kawalek, 2018. "Understanding big data analytics capabilities in supply chain management: Unravelling the issues, challenges and implications for practice." Transportation Research Part E: Logistics and Transportation Review, 114. pp. 416–436. ISSN 1366-5545.

5 Abramowicz, W., Paschke, A., 2019. Business Information Systems Workshops: BIS 2018 International Workshops, Berlin, Germany, July 18–20, 2018, Revised Papers.

6 Riepl, W., 2012. CRISP-DM: Ein Standard-Prozess-Modell für Data Mining. Stat. Dresd. URL https://statistik-dresden.de/archives/1128.

7 De Mauro, A., Greco, M., Grimaldi, M., Ritala, P., 2017. Human Resources for Big Data Professions: A systematic Classification of Job Roles and Required

Skill Sets. URL https://www.researchgate.net/publication/317423968_Human_resources_for_Big_Data_professions_A_systematic_classification_of_job_roles_and_required_skill_sets/link/59a29d38aca2726b90267b5d/download.

8 Conway, D., 2013. Big Data [sorry] & Data Science: What Does a Data Scientist Do? URL https://de.slideshare.net/datasciencelondon/big-data-sorry-data-science-what-does-a-data-scientist-do.

9 Peterson, K., n. d. ORION Backgrounder [WWW Document]. Press. URL https://www.pressroom.ups.com/pressroom/ContentDetailsViewer.page?ConceptType=Factsheets&id=1426321616277-282 (accessed 12.12.19).

10 Mrozek, T., Koch, J., Götte, A., 2020. Digital Transformation Study.

Artificial Intelligence: Supply Chains will never be the same

1 Stefik, M., 1985. Strategic computing at DARPA: overview and assessment. Commun. ACM 28, 690–704. https://doi.org/10.1145/3894.3896.

2 Ibid.

3 Mrozek, T., Koch, J., 2018. Transformation: Der Weg zur digital integrierten Supply Chain. h&z Unternehmensberatung AG. URL https://huz.de/2018/08/21/digitale-supply-chain-2/.

4 Shorten, C., 2018. Machine Learning vs. Deep Learning. Medium. URL https://towardsdatascience.com/machine-learning-vs-deep-learning-62137a1c9842.

5 Salian, I., 2018. NVIDIA Blog: Supervised Vs. Unsupervised. Off. NVIDIA Blog. URL https://blogs.nvidia.com/blog/2018/08/02/supervised-unsupervised-learning/ (accessed 12.12.19).

6 Ibid.

7 Goasduff, L., 2019. Top Trends on the Gartner Hype Cycle for Artificial Intelligence, 2019. URL //www.gartner.com/smarterwithgartner/top-trends-on-the-gartner-hype-cycle-for-artificial-intelligence-2019/.

8 Gesing, B., Peterson, S.J., Michelsen, D.D., 2018. Artificial Intelligence in Logistics. URL https://www.logistics.dhl/content/dam/dhl/global/core/documents/pdf/glo-core-trend-report-artificial-intelligence.pdf.

9 Ibid.

10 Mrozek, T., Koch, J., 2018. Transformation: Der Weg zur digital integrierten Supply Chain. h&z Unternehmensberatung AG. URL https://huz.de/2018/08/21/digitale-supply-chain-2/.

11 Artificial Intelligence Market Expected to Surge, 2019. Supply Demand Chain Exec. URL https://www.sdcexec.com/software-technology/news/21074393/artificial-intelligence-market-expected-to-surge.

12 O'Marah, K., Chen, X., 2016. Future of Supply Chain. URL www.scmworld.com/wp-content/uploads/2017/07/Future_of_Supply_Chain_2016_.pdf

13 Shah, S., 2019. Merck sets the next destination for its "self-driving" business. URL http://www.i-cio.com/strategy/digitalization/item/merck-sets-the-next-destination-for-its-self-driving-supply-chain.

14 Ray, T., 2019. Keras inventor Chollet charts a new direction for AI: a Q&A. ZDNet. URL https://www.zdnet.com/article/keras-creator-chollets-new-direction-for-ai-a-q-a/.
15 Yao, M., 2017. Understanding the limits of deep learning. URL https://venturebeat.com/2017/04/02/understanding-the-limits-of-deep-learning/.

Digital Procurement: A key driver for performance improvement

1 Ariba, 2019. How OMV AG is Digitally Transforming its Supplier Relationship Management. URL https://www.ariba.com/de-de/resources/library/library-pages/how-omv-ag-is-digitally-transforming-its-supplier-relationship-management#.
2 Ariba, 2019. How OMV AG is Digitally Transforming its Supplier Relationship Management. URL https://www.ariba.com/de-de/resources/library/library-pages/how-omv-ag-is-digitally-transforming-its-supplier-relationship-management#.
3 h&z Unternehmensberatung AG, 09.2019. h&z Magazin: Business-Transformation in der Praxis.

Future Supply Chain Planning: Faster and smarter

1 Coldrick, A., Ling, D., Turner, C., 2003. Integrated Decision Making—The Choices 12.
2 Alicke, K., Hoberg, K., Rachor, J., 2019. The Supply Chain Planner of the Future. URL https://www.supplychain247.com/article/the_supply_chain_planner_of_the_future.
3 Hippold, S., 2019. The 7 Dimensions of Digital Supply Chain Planning. URL https://www.gartner.com/smarterwithgartner/the-7-dimensions-of-digital-supply-chain-planning/.

Logistics Today and Tomorrow

1 Keller, S., 2019a. Logistikbranche in Deutschland—Umsatz. Statista. URL https://de.statista.com/statistik/daten/studie/166970/umfrage/umsatz-der-logistikbranche-in-deutschland/.
2 Keller, S., 2019b. Marktvolumen des Logistikmarktes in Europa. Statista. URL https://de.statista.com/statistik/daten/studie/204132/umfrage/volumen-des-logistikmarktes-in-europa/.
3 Möger, M., 2018. Die digitalisierte Supply Chain—Fraunhofer SCS und Fraunhofer IIS auf der LogiMAT 2018. Fraunhofer-Arbeitsgruppe Für Supply Chain Serv. SCS. URL https://www.scs.fraunhofer.de/de/presse/pressemitteilungen/20180215_LogiMAT2018.html.

4 Schiller, K., 2018. Was sind Smart Contracts? Definition und Erklärung. Block-chainwelt. URL https://blockchainwelt.de/smart-contracts-vertrag-blockchain/.

5 Morgan, B., 2018. 5 Examples Of How AI Can Be Used Across The Supply Chain. Forbes. URL https://www.forbes.com/sites/blakemorgan/2018/09/17/5-examples-of-how-ai-can-be-used-across-the-supply-chain/.

6 Sorokanich, L., 2019. This cold-storage company that works with Walmart and McDonald's cut its energy consumption 34% and saves millions of dollars a year. Fast Co. URL https://www.fastcompany.com/90299025/lineage-logistics-most-innovative-companies-2019.

Supply Chain Visibility: Connecting the dots

1 Peterson, A., 2018. 4 Reasons to Move to B2B Cloud Inventory Management. URL https://blog.apruve.com/4-reasons-to-move-b2b-cloud-inventory-management.

2 Businesswire, 2019. NTT Group führt Compliance-Management-Lösung mit Robotic Process Automation (RPA) ein. URL https://www.businesswire.com/news/home/20191218005813/de/

3 Geodis, 2017. Supply Chain Worldwide Survey.

4 Zetes, 2017. Manufacturers want supply chain visibility and collaboration; what's holding them back? URL https://www.zetes.com/themes/zetes/files/pdf/white_papers/REPmanufEN-LRES_g.pdf?utm_campaign=EN-WHITE-PA PER-DOWNLOAD-FROM-WEBSITE&utm_medium=email&utm_source=El oqua&elqTrackId=7ba7038b2b394eb8bb56b6eeb3d5160c&elq=78b1d4a6f66b 4f27ae773fce37528cd7&elqaid=2633&elqat=1&elqCampaignId=.

5 Synchrono, 2016. Supply Chain Visibility and the Bottom-line—Supply Chain 24/7. URL https://www.supplychain247.com/article/supply_chain_visibility_a nd_the_bottom_line/synchr.

6 Reidy, S., 2019. How to choose a supply chain visibility provider? Arviem Cargo Monit. URL https://arviem.com/choosing-supply-chain-visibility-software-pro vider/ (accessed 12.12.19).

Being a Leader in a Digital Supply Chain

1 Autor, D. H., 2015. Why Are There Still So Many Jobs? The History and Future of Workplace Automation. URL https://economics.mit.edu/files/11563.

2 Kane, G. C. et al., 2019. How Digital Leadership Is(n't) Different. URL https://sloanreview.mit.edu/article/how-digital-leadership-isnt-different/.

3 Mrozek, T., Koch, J., Götte, A., 2020. Digital Transformation Study.

4 O'Marah, K., 2016. Future Of Work: Four Supply Chain Careers For 2025. URL https://www.forbes.com/sites/kevinomarah/2016/12/15/future-of-work-four-supply-chain-careers-for-2025/#3d252b281079.

Cultural transformation: The heart and soul of digitalization

1 Mrozek, T., Koch, J., 2018. Transformation: Der Weg zur digital integrierten Supply Chain. h&z Unternehmensberatung AG. URL https://huz.de/2018/08/21/digitale-supply-chain-2/.
2 Mrozek, T., Koch, J., 2018. Transformation: Der Weg zur digital integrierten Supply Chain. h&z Unternehmensberatung AG. URL https://huz.de/2018/08/21/digitale-supply-chain-2/.
3 McCracken, K., 2018. Transforming culture at Microsoft: Satya Nadella sets a new tone. URL https://www.intheblack.com/articles/2018/06/01/satya-nadella-transforming-culture-microsoft.
4 Mrozek, T., Koch, J., 2018. Transformation: Der Weg zur digital integrierten Supply Chain. h&z Unternehmensberatung AG. URL https://huz.de/2018/08/21/digitale-supply-chain-2/.
5 Sagmeister, S., Business Culture Design, Campus 2016.

Digital Transformation Office: The engine for success

1 Harvey Nash/KPMG, 2018. CIO Survey 2018. URL https://www.harveynash.com/usa/news-and-insights/US_CIO_survey_2018.pdf.
2 Wade, M., 2017. Standing Ovation: McLaren Puts the Digital Orchestra into Action LinkedIn. URL https://www.linkedin.com/pulse/standing-ovation-mclaren-puts-digital-orchestra-action-michael-wade/.
3 Flemming, S., Grimm, F., Früh, F., 2018. Bitkom Digital Office Index 89. URL bitkom.org/Bitkom/Publikationen/Bitkom-Digital-Office-Index-2018.html.
4 Peladeau, P., Acker, O., 2019. Have we reached "peak" chief digital officer? strategy++business. URL https://www.strategy-business.com/blog/Have-we-reached-peak-chief-digital-officer?gko=9ce66.

Getting it done: Proven strategies and a survival guide

1 Robinson, H., 2019. Why do most transformations fail? A conversation with Harry Robinson. URL https://www.mckinsey.com/business-functions/transformation/our-insights/why-do-most-transformations-fail-a-conversation-with-harry-robinson.
2 Rogers, B., 2016. Why 84% Of Companies Fail At Digital Transformation. URL https://www.forbes.com/sites/brucerogers/2016/01/07/why-84-of-companies-fail-at-digital-transformation/#337af62b397b.
3 Consultancy.uk, 2015. Two thirds of digital transformation projects fail. URL https://www.consultancy.uk/news/2656/two-thirds-of-digital-transformation-projects-fail.
4 Bodkin, H., 2016. NHS email blunder clogs up system after message sent to 840,000 employees. The Telegraph.